More than PETTICOATS

Remarkable North Carolina Women

Scotti Kent

D1557650

TWODOT

For my parents,

who instilled in me an appreciation

for the richness of the past.

A · TWODOT · BOOK

© 2000 Falcon® Publishing Inc., Helena, Montana.
Printed in Canada.

1 2 3 4 5 6 7 8 9 0 TP 04 03 02 01 00 99

All rights reserved, including the right to reproduce this book or any parts thereof in any form, except brief quotations in a review.

Cover photo courtesy the North Carolina Collection, University of North Crolina Library at Chapel Hill.

Library of Congress Cataloging-in-Publication Data

Kent, Scotti, 1950-.
    More than petticoats : remarkable North Carolina women / Scotti Kent.
        p.   cm.
    Includes bibliographical references and index.
    ISBN 1-56044-900-4 (pbk.)
    1. Women—North Carolina—Biography. 2. North Carolina—Biography.
I. Title.
CT3260.K46 2000
920.72'09756—dc21   99-044216

CONTENTS

ACKNOWLEDGMENTS

I have the utmost respect and appreciation for the people listed below, who shared information and stories, offered encouragement, and reviewed parts of my manuscript for accuracy.

Phyllis H. Crain, Ed. D., Executive Director, Crossnore School, Crossnore

Rev. Michael Feely, Greeneville, Tennessee

Jean Johnson, Asheville

Bill Millsaps, Robbinsville

Joseph Mitchell, former Executive Director, Crossnore School, Crossnore

Milton Ready, Ph.D., Professor of History, University of North Carolina, Asheville

Bo Taylor, Museum of the Cherokee, Cherokee

Charles W. Wadelington, Minority Interpretations Specialist, North Carolina Department of Cultural Resources, Division of Archives and History, Historic Sites Section, Raleigh

I also deeply appreciate everyone who agreed to be interviewed about a specific subject. They are mentioned by name in the appropriate chapters.

My special thanks goes to the librarians at Pack Memorial Library, Asheville; University of North Carolina at Chapel Hill; North Carolina Division of Archives and History; and Winston-Salem State University.

Finally, I thank educator Alice Hall for encouraging me to become a writer in my earliest years of life; my editor, Charlene Patterson, for her insightful questions and suggestions; and my husband, Don, for his unfailing support and companionship.

INTRODUCTION

North Carolina boasts a history that spans thousands of years. From the days when Native Americans hunted its forests and fished its streams alone, its story extends to colonial times, through revolutions, secessions, and two world wars, to the cusp of the future. Written accounts of the area date back to the 1540s, when Spanish explorer Hernando de Soto arrived on the scene. However, archaeologists believe North Carolina's first colonists preceded de Soto by more than twelve thousand years. These prehistoric North Carolinians lived in small camps, relocating with the changing seasons in their search for deer, elk, and bear. They were the ancestors of tribes now known as the Catawba, Cherokee, and Creek Indians.

With such a rich heritage, it is not surprising that North Carolina today is a complex, colorful place. Like a handmade Native American basket, a patchwork quilt stitched by European pioneers, or an intricately beaded African necklace, it is composed of diverse elements, joined together and intertwined.

Over the years, women have woven their spirits deep into the design of this remarkable state. The threads of their lives connect its three distinct geographical regions and bind centuries of history to each other. Yet, in spite of their profound contributions, the women of North Carolina, like their sisters in other states, appear but rarely in history books produced during the first two centuries of our nation's life. What has passed for "American history" is largely the story of white European men, with an occasional stray reference to the existence of other groups.

As I was gathering information for this book, I mentioned its title to a friend. Clearly feeling neglected, he commented, "Maybe your next book can be on remarkable North Carolina *men*." I did not know what to say. I had just come from the North Carolina Room of the public library, with its shelves and shelves of thick tomes on the history of the state, filled with chapter after chapter about men. I had browsed through the indexes of these impressive volumes, searching for the names of women. The "pickin's" were mighty slim.

To those who imply that we have gone off the deep end in our attempt to bring women closer to the forefront of history, I can think of only one response: We're still in the "shallows." The same is true for efforts to highlight Native American and African American contributions.

More than Petticoats: Remarkable North Carolina Women celebrates individuals of different ethnic backgrounds who inhabited various regions of the state during assorted historical periods. By necessity, my choices for the book were based partly on the availability of information on the people I wanted to include. In an effort to control the size of the book, I limited the chapters to fourteen, and, in the tradition of other books in the *More than Petticoats* series, required that my subjects had been born before 1900. Even so, I had to omit countless women who were every bit as remarkable as those I featured.

Another issue worth mentioning is the challenge of writing about the past from the perspective of the present. Although it may be possible to write history without allowing any intrusion from the current day, I do not make that claim for this book. Rather, it is a blend of past and present points of view. In some cases, my goal is to make readers feel they are standing right beside the woman, seeing what she saw, knowing what she knew. At other times, situations are described from a more contemporary, objective angle.

My most important overall purpose is to present these fourteen North Carolina women as individuals, to allow readers to relate to them one-on-one. To some extent, they were products of their era and their environment, as are we all. Yet I hope you will find, as I did, a moment or two of commonality and an understanding of how the current generation has built upon the compassion and courage these women demonstrated, and how we might carry those qualities forward. It is this ability of the human spirit to connect to the past while linking to the future that I find truly remarkable.

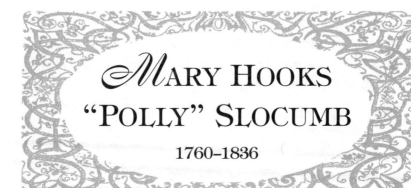

MARY HOOKS "POLLY" SLOCUMB
1760–1836

Heroine of Moore's Creek Bridge

One evening in late February 1776, a band of nearly one thousand British Loyalists assembled about six miles from Moore's Creek Bridge on North Carolina's coastal plain. The men, under the command of Lieutenant Colonel Donald MacDonald, had gathered in response to a call from the royal governor of the colony, Josiah Martin. Martin had been exiled by "evil, pernicious, and traitorous" radicals who had set up a Provincial Congress in North Carolina to rule in his stead. From his place of refuge aboard a British warship anchored off the coast, he had summoned "His Majesty's subjects" to rally around the royal standard.

Even though New England was already in rebellion, as evidenced by battles fought at Lexington and Concord almost a full year earlier, Martin was certain he could bring the Southern colonies back in line if he acted quickly and decisively.

The Loyalists nearing Moore's Creek Bridge that February evening knew Patriot forces waited just ahead, but they had already changed course once to avoid tangling with a colonial army. MacDonald had learned that those same colonial troops were now headed toward his current position. His militia was trapped. To make

NATIONAL PARK SERVICE

*Monument and graves of Ezekiel and Mary Slocumb
at Moore's Creek battleground*

matters worse, the members of his Loyalist band had not proved very loyal at all. In fact, desertion had been the order of the day. The faithful group remaining at MacDonald's side consisted primarily of Scottish Highlanders, and many of them were new to the country and not terribly sure why they were fighting.

At the council of war that cold winter's night, MacDonald was showing strain. Nearly seventy years old, he was exhausted and ill with a fever. He advised against attacking the Patriots. His Highlanders, however, were not to be dissuaded. They voted to wage a frontal assault.

Sixty-five miles away, Mary Hooks Slocumb tossed and turned in her bed. Her husband, Ezekiel, had left their plantation two days earlier with more than eighty men. The group had been in high spirits, looking forward to helping Colonel Caswell crush the Loyalists. On his hat, Ezekiel wore the familiar silver crescent blazing the words "Liberty or Death." Around his shoulders lay the warm cloak Mary herself had made him not long ago.

In Mrs. Elizabeth Ellett's book *Women of the American Revolution*, published in 1850, the following is presented as an excerpt from Mary's own diary: "As I lay—whether waking or sleeping I know not—I had a dream; yet it was not all a dream. I saw distinctly a body wrapped in my husband's guard cloak, bloody—dead—and others dead and wounded on the ground around him."

Still under the spell of the disturbing images, Mary jumped out of bed and rushed in the direction in which the vision had appeared. She ran into a wall. Stunned, she glanced wildly about, certain the bloody body must be nearby. "I raised the light; everything was still and quiet. My child was sleeping. . . . If ever I felt fear, it was at that moment. Seated on the bed, I reflected a few moments and said aloud: 'I must go to him!'"

Mary told her servant that she could not sleep and would ride down the road. The woman was instructed to lock the door and look after Mary's baby. Mary saddled a sure-footed mare and rode at full gallop into the blustery, black night.

Just after midnight, an advance party of Scottish warriors, broadswords at the ready, made their way through thickets and across swampy ground toward the Patriot tents, where fires burned brightly. To their surprise, the camp was deserted. The way seemed clear for them to proceed to Wilmington.

Beginning with a single note, the plaintive squall of the bag-pipes soon swelled to fill the air. In the frost-tipped woods of the New World, by the dark, sluggish waters of Moore's Creek, the pipes and drums of the Celts set the marching pace. A signal was given by Alexander McLean who had taken the place of the ailing MacDonald. Three cheers rang out, and the Loyalists rushed the bridge.

As Mary Slocumb rode through the woods, she heard a sound like thunder in the distance. Realizing the battle must be going on at that very moment, she urged her mare forward, faster than ever.

At Moore's Creek, the scene was bloody indeed. The Patriots, more than one thousand in number, had pulled up the bridge's planks and slathered soft soap and tallow on the girders. They had then hidden behind trees and embankments built during the night. Colonel Lillington, with 150 men, waited on the east side of the bridge, and Colonel Caswell, with 850 men, camped on the west side.

When McLean and his soldiers dashed forward with their battle cry and broadswords, the Patriots opened fire with their muskets and cannons, driving back the head of the column. The Scots lost their footing on the slippery, partly dismantled bridge. They toppled into the cold, murky water where they drowned or crumpled to the ground from exhaustion on the other side. McLean fell, fatally wounded.

Outflanked and deprived of their leader, the Loyalists scattered in every direction. In a few moments, the first battle of the

American Revolution in the South was over.

By this time, Mary Slocumb had arrived on the scene. Elizabeth Ellett again quoted:

> I know the spot, the very trees . . . as if I had seen it a
> thousand times. I had seen it in my dream all night. . . .
> There, wrapped in his bloody guard cloak, was my
> husband's body. How I passed the few yards from my
> saddle to this place, I never knew. I remember uncovering
> his head and seeing a face clothed with gore from a dreadful wound across the temple. I put my hand on the bloody
> face; 'twas warm.

Trembling, Mary took a small camp kettle, filled it with water, and poured some into the mouth of the man she assumed was her dear Ezekiel. Gently, she bathed his face with the rest of the water. To her shock and relief, the injured man was not her husband at all, but one of the men who had ridden away with him two days before. Her husband had placed his cloak over the man to keep him warm. Still not knowing Ezekiel's fate, Mary used a piece of trouser leg and a handful of heart leaves to dress and bind her neighbor's wounds. She then set about tending to the other soldiers as best she could.

Suddenly, she looked up and saw Ezekiel "as muddy as a ditcher" standing before her. Mary could not bring herself to tell him what had brought her to his side. She provided first aid and shared in the celebration of victory, then mounted her horse to return home. She headed back through the dark woods, her heart far lighter than it had been the night before.

The Battle of Moore's Creek is hailed today as the first decisive victory of the colonists against Great Britain in the South. An article about the Moore's Creek Bridge Historic Site sums up the encounter as follows: "Though the battle was a small one, the implications were large. The victory demonstrated the surprising Patriot strength in the country side, discouraged the growth of Loyalist sentiment in the Carolinas, and spurred revolutionary feeling throughout the Colonies."

Mary Hooks Slocumb is best remembered for her frightening vision and dramatic midnight ride. Her bravery and attention to the wounded are chronicled in Mary Lewis Wyche's book *The History of Nursing in North Carolina*. Yet, like most women of her time, Mary had to put her courage and resourcefulness to use every day in order to simply survive.

Born in 1760, Mary Hooks was the daughter of Thomas and Anna Bellotte Hooks. She spent her early childhood in Bertie County, North Carolina, less than twenty miles inland from the Albemarle Sound. An area first inhabited by the Chowanoc, Moratoc, and Mangoak Indians, the county was interlaced with fields, forests, and broad, deep rivers like the Chowan, Roanoke, and Cashie.

When Mary was ten, she moved with her family to Duplin County on the coastal plain, joining the Welsh, English, Scotch-Irish, German, and Swiss settlers who had come during the 1730s. In those days, a great many Duplin County residents were involved in harvesting rosin from the pine forests to make tar, pitch, and turpentine. These products were floated down the Northeast Cape Fear River to Wilmington on large, log rafts.

As a young girl, Mary learned typical domestic duties like carding, spinning, weaving, and sewing. She also learned how to ride a horse, shoot a pistol, and manage a farm.

Mary Hooks married Ezekiel Slocumb when both were in their teens. The couple settled in what is now Wayne County on a plantation Ezekiel had inherited from his father. Their honeymoon was brief, as the groom was already one of the light horse troops who acted as scouts in the area. Their mission was to prevent Tory uprisings in their neck of the woods. When Ezekiel was gone—which was much of the time—Mary ran the plantation, serving as both master and mistress. Ellett reported in *Women of the American Revolution*: "She used to say, laughingly, that she had done in those perilous days all that a man ever did except 'maul rails,' and to take away even that exception, she went out one day and 'split a few.' And this was to keep up all during the long drawn out years of the Revolution."

Near the end of April 1781, Mary found herself playing hostess to an infamous English officer named Banastre Tarleton who was well known and hated by the colonists for massacring American soldiers who tried to surrender to him at Waxhaw. When the British marched to Virginia under Lord Cornwallis, the Slocumb farm was right at the end of their march. Tarleton announced that he, his aides, and nearly 250 soldiers would be taking advantage of Mary Slocumb's hospitality for awhile. Just a short distance away, Ezekiel and friends were actually engaged in a skirmish against the Tories.

Colonel Tarleton asked Mary if her husband was a rebel. Mary replied that he was in the army of his country, fighting against invaders, and was therefore not a rebel.

"A friend of his country will be the friend of the king, our master," said the Tory.

Mary's acid reply came quickly. "In this country, only slaves acknowledge a master."

At another time, Tarleton remarked that the officers of his army would undoubtedly receive large possessions of the conquered American provinces.

"The only land in these United States which will ever remain in possession of a British officer will measure but six feet by two," Mary retorted.

The presence of the enemy did not frighten Mary, but she was concerned for the safety of Ezekiel and his companions. What if they returned home while the Loyalists were there? The troops had pitched tents and set up camp in the Slocumb's orchard and field.

Quick-thinking Mary posted a trusted slave known as "Big George" at the edge of the yard to keep watch. As Ezekiel and his companions drew near, George warned them. They turned around and fled in a hail of balls from the Redcoats' guns.

Following the war, Ezekiel and Mary—who was now called "Polly" by many of her friends—led a less traumatic life. Ezekiel served as a member of the House of Commons of North Carolina between 1812 and 1818. Their son, Jesse, was elected a member of Congress in 1817 and served until he died in 1821. The Slocumbs also had two daughters: Sarah and Susannah.

Mary Hooks Slocumb died on March 6, 1836. Her dear Ezekiel joined her on July 4, 1840, exactly sixty-four years after fellow North Carolinians William Hooper, Joseph Hewes, and John Penn signed America's Declaration of Independence.

Today, the Slocumbs' graves lie just below a monument erected in 1907 at the Moore's Creek battleground, now a national military park in Currie, North Carolina. Fashioned from Italian marble, the statue depicts a woman holding a wreath and wearing a long, loose-fitting toga-style garment. Among the inscriptions on the monument are the following words:

> This monument was erected by the Moore's Creek Monumental Association in the year 1907. To the honored memory of the Heroic Women of the Lower Cape Fear during the American Revolution 1775–1781. Most honored of the names recorded by this historic association is that of Mary Slocumb, wife of Lieutenant Slocumb . . . Her heroism and self-sacrifice place her high on the pages of history and should awaken in successive generations true patriotism and love of country.

These words are a fitting tribute to a woman whose frightful premonition of her husband's death proved false and whose dream of liberty for her country came true.✤

AUTHOR'S NOTE: Many serious historians believe that Mary Slocumb's ride and her encounter with Colonel Tarleton are legends rather than historical fact. Elizabeth Ellett did not reveal her source for the account presented in her book, although Louis T. Moore, Chairman of the New Hanover Historical Commission, stated in 1956 that "the record was preserved by her [Mary Slocumb's] family." All subsequent versions of the story have been derived from Ellett's book. Numerous details in Ellett's account conflict with official records of the battle of Moore's Creek Bridge and other credible sources, including dates inscribed on the Slocumbs' tombstones.

In spite of this, the Mooresville, North Carolina, chapter of the Daughters of the American Revolution is named for Mary. She is praised in the inscription on the monument at Moore's Creek Bridge. Her story has been printed in respected books, newspapers, and magazines. No one disputes that Mary and Ezekiel Slocumb existed. Although there is no evidence that Ezekiel fought at Moore's Creek Bridge, his name is recorded in the North Carolina Pension Roll of the U.S. War Department as a soldier from North Carolina who fought in the American Revolution. His post-war service in the General Assembly is also documented. Mary is viewed as a symbol of the patriotism and sacrifice of the women of the coastal plains.

Susan Twitty

1763–1825

Defender of Graham's Fort

*S*eventeen-year-old Susan Twitty wasn't sure which noise was loudest—the intermittent *bang! pop! bang!* of the gunfire, the cries of the frightened children, or the pounding of her own heart.

She forced herself to stay calm as she helped her older brother, William, reload his rifle. This was the safest place they could be— holed up in the large, hewn-log house belonging to her stepfather, Colonel William Graham. The biggest, strongest structure in the area, "Graham's Fort" was the designated place of refuge for the women, children, and elderly of the community. In the event of an attack by Indians or Tories, they knew to run there for protection.

The loyal subjects of England, called "Tories" or "Loyalists," were at war on American soil with rebellious Patriots who sought to break free and "form a more perfect union." The fighting had offi- cially begun in April of 1775 when shots were fired at Lexington and Concord, Massachusetts.

At first, the revolution didn't have much of an effect on the people who lived in the foothills of the Blue Ridge Mountains in western North Carolina. However, in 1780 they were forced to sit up and take notice. The war in the North had reached a stalemate, and the British decided to pursue their objectives in the South. There, they were certain, huge numbers of Loyalists would step forward in support of King George. In fact, there were quite a few British sympathizers in what later became North Carolina's Cleveland and Rutherford counties.

Once pressed into duty, the Tories began roaming the countryside, terrorizing the Patriots' families and stealing or destroying their belongings. Not to be outdone, the Patriots took to traveling the backwoods in small bands, hoping to beat the Loyalists at their own game.

That bright September morning in 1780, Susan Twitty and her neighbors had barricaded themselves in Graham's Fort, having been being warned that a band of Tory raiders was on its way. Not long after they barred the door, the enemy arrived, their horses prancing and snorting in the crisp fall air. Susan peered through a crack between the logs. With a sinking heart, she realized the Tories numbered twenty or more. The helpless people crouching on the floor inside the fort had just three men to protect them: Susan's stepfather, Colonel William Graham; her brother, William Twitty; and David Dickey.

To be truthful, Susan considered herself a fourth defender. Years ago, she had insisted her big brother teach her to load and fire a musket, so she would be ready if Indians or Redcoats threatened her. She now stood beside nineteen-year-old William, prepared to fight.

"I order you to surrender in the name of the King!" shouted one of the Tory soldiers.

Susan and her brother exchanged glances. Colonel Graham finished loading his rifle. David Dickey raised his gun, easing the end of the muzzle through a small opening between the logs. A child whimpered and was gently quieted by her mother. For several seconds, the heavy silence was broken only by the raucous cry of a crow and a horse's nervous whinny.

Then the Tory officer barked an order, and the air exploded in a barrage of gunfire. A woman screamed. Round lead balls, some the size of quarters, zipped through the cracks in the fort's log walls, whizzing above the heads of the terrified occupants.

The Tory officer demanded that the people inside Graham's Fort surrender as his troops primed and reloaded their weapons. In response, William Twitty fired his rifle, which prompted the Tories to unleash another volley.

As William reloaded, Susan kept watch. Suddenly, one of the enemy soldiers, later identified as John Burke, ran right up to the fort! He thrust the muzzle of his musket through one of the openings between the logs. With a cry, Susan grabbed her brother's arm and jerked him down a split second before Burke pulled the trigger. The deadly ball lodged itself harmlessly in the opposite wall.

Susan popped up in time to see the Tory soldier not far away, engaged in the twelve-step process he had to go through before he could fire his gun again. She told her brother that now was his chance to shoot the soldier.

Lutie Andrews McCorkle described what happened next in *Old Time Stories of the Old North State*:

> *Bang!* went William's gun, and the bold Tory fell over, shot through the head. Susan unbarred the door, darted into the yard, picked up the young Tory's rifle and ammunition, and with a shower of Tory bullets raining around her, rushed back into the house.

Once inside the fort, Susan continued assisting the men and even got off a few shots herself.

"With one killed and three wounded, the Tories relinquished the assault and retreated," reported Elizabeth Simpson in a 1972 article for *The State*. "Colonel Graham, anticipating their return, gathered up his family and friends and departed for more distant quarters. Later he was brought the news that the reinforced Tories had returned and devastated Graham's Fort."

The fort may have been destroyed, but Susan Twitty's bravery and determination under fire had helped ensure the safety of her kinfolk and neighbors.

Born July 3, 1763, Susan, who signed her will "Susanna" but was called "Susan" in nearly every published account of her life, was the daughter of William and Susannah Twitty. Susan grew up caring for farm animals, making soap from melted lard, and helping her mother keep the family fed and clothed.

Her father met with an unfortunate end, as described by William Twitty Carpenter in *The Heritage of Rutherford County*:

Back in the late 1700s William Twitty signed on to help cut a 30-foot right-of-way from Otter Creek, Tennessee, to Boonesboro, Kentucky. There were 30 men in the party under direction of Daniel Boone. This work was to be done for the Transylvania company.

Twitty never made it back to North Carolina. In March of 1775, he was killed by Indians near the Kentucky River. Thus at the age of twelve, Susan was left fatherless, along with her brothers and sisters, William, Allen, Russell, Mary, Arabella, Bellariah, and Charlotte. It was during this period in her life that Susan coaxed William into teaching her, in McCorkle's words, "to ride the swiftest horse without a saddle and to shoot his Deckard rifle with true aim."

In time, Susan's mother married distinguished landowner William Graham from Virginia. A prominent member of the community, Colonel Graham served as a delegate to the Fifth Provincial Congress, where he was instrumental in forming North Carolina's first state constitution. As a member of the county militia, he had seen action in the Snow campaign against the Cherokee Indians and against the Tories at Moore's Creek Bridge in 1776. That same year, he led a regiment to Charleston, South Carolina, in an attempt to rescue that proud city from a British invasion. However, as Clarence Griffin reported in his *History of Old Tryon and Rutherford Counties*, "they found the city so completely infested by the British Army that they could not render assistance to the American garrison and retired."

Susan Twitty grew up close to the border between North and South Carolina. In the distance, the foothills of the Blue Ridge Mountains rose against a vast, pure sky. Some say there were "few or no small trees" among the virgin timber that reached two hundred feet into the air. It was hard to decide which was more dazzling: autumn's brilliant reds and golds, or the vivid pinks and purples that covered the landscape in spring.

In October of 1780, one foothill in particular became more significant than the others to Susan—indeed, to the entire nation. Called King's Mountain, the heavily-forested ridge straddled the line between the two Carolinas. That fall, with its massive oaks, walnuts, and hickories clothed in fiery fall splendor, it more than deserved its royal name. And although it was only sixty feet high, defending it would prove too tall an order for the British.

Charleston had fallen, and thousands of Patriot leaders and soldiers had been imprisoned. British commander Lord Cornwallis sent Major Patrick Ferguson deep into North Carolina to gather supporters of the Crown into a Tory militia. Ferguson had considerable success in his mission. However, his membership drive failed to entice the "over-mountain" men.

The descendants of Celts, Britons, Normans, Romans, Anglo-Saxons, and stone-age tribes of Ireland, the over-mountain men had settled Rutherford County in the early 1700s. With the Cherokee Indians to the west and the Catawba Indians to the east, they were used to fighting to acquire and keep what they had. They were not impressed by the King's edicts, and they certainly didn't intend to let someone on the other side of an ocean tell them how to live. Even their religion encouraged toughness and endurance. The Presbyterian Church drew heavily from the Old Testament and was quite comfortable invoking the "Lord of battle."

Although the over-mountain men were rough and ready, they preferred to spend most of their time cultivating their farms, ignoring the British presence. Occasionally, however, they engaged in minor skirmishes with the Loyalists. This angered Major Ferguson, who issued a threat described by Peggy Beach in an article posted on the Cleveland County, North Carolina, website:

> In late September, Ferguson camped at Gilbert Town (near present day Rutherfordton). He sent a message to Colonel Isaac Shelby, whom he considered to be the leader of the "backwater men." The message said that if Shelby and his men did not stop their opposition to the British, Ferguson would march his army over the mountains, hang their leaders and "lay the country waste with fire and sword."

No doubt Susan Twitty bristled when she heard about the threat and cheered when she found out how the mountaineers responded. Over a thousand men, varying in age from sixteen to sixty, assembled at Sycamore Shoals, Tennessee. In an inspiring address, Reverend Samuel Doak urged them to "wield the sword of the Lord and Gideon." Motivated, they marched off in search of "Fierce Ferguson" and his army, picking up additional Patriots as they went. Their quest led them to King's Mountain, where Ferguson had camped on his way to Charlotte to join Cornwallis.

Susan's heart was filled with pride as she watched William and her stepfather ride off to battle in the early morning rain on October 6. She was pleased by the wet weather, for she knew it would allow the Patriots to stay on horseback most of the way up the hill. There would be no dust to alert Ferguson to their presence. She also knew that when they got within a mile of the Tories, they could easily hide among the trees.

Like Susan's stepfather and brother, the vast majority of the Patriots were expert marksmen, skilled at hitting fast-moving game with deadly accuracy. The Loyalists, on the other hand, were handicapped by a fighting style which called for them to shoot as a group then charge with bayonets extended. Their Brown Bess muskets took a long time to load and frequently misfired. Susan had heard it said that the British didn't aim their weapons, they just pointed them in a general direction and hoped for the best.

She could imagine what the battle on King's Mountain would be like. She was certain the mountain men would prevail. It troubled her, though, that Ferguson had managed to raise nearly a thousand Tories from among her own countrymen. Her brother and Colonel Graham would not be killing "the British" that day. In a very real sense, they would be shooting their own people. Furthermore, Susan suspected it would do no good for the Tories to wave a white flag. Patriot blood was still boiling over the massacre at Waxhaw, where British General Tarleton had willfully slaughtered colonists who were trying to surrender.

Susan's imagination proved quite accurate. Ferguson himself was fatally wounded. According to Peggy Beach, "225 Loyalists were killed, 163 were wounded, 716 were taken prisoner. 28 Patriots were killed and 68 were wounded." She described the impact the battle had on the revolution:

The battle fought on October 7, 1780, destroyed the left wing of Cornwallis' army and effectively ended Loyalist ascendance in the Carolinas. The victory halted the British advance into North Carolina, forced Lord Cornwallis to retreat from Charlotte into South Carolina, and gave General Nathanael Greene the opportunity to reorganize the American Army.

At the end of the revolution, Susan married John Miller .His parents, David Miller and Mary Kerr, had sailed from Ireland to America around 1764, when John was a young boy. Susan and John built a home on a farm provided by John's father.

In *Tar Heel Women*, published in 1947, Lou Rogers reported that John Miller represented Rutherford County in the legislature in the early 1800s and died while attending court in Asheville in 1807. This is supported, at least in part, by a letter written by family historian Horace L. Carpenter in 1951.

According to Twitty family researcher Carol Middleton, Susan and John Miller had at least one daughter, Mary, and one son, William, who died at age twelve. Other accounts state that a son, W. J. T. Miller, represented Rutherford County in the legislature from 1836 to 1840. Susan Twitty Miller's will directed that "John Twitty" should receive some land and two cows. Later, the will referred to "my son John Miller Twitty" and "my daughter Susanna Lowry." It is likely that "John Miller Twitty" should have read "John Twitty Miller."

There is also some confusion about Susan Twitty Miller's year of death. Her will was dated March 26, 1825, and McCorkle states that she died that same year. The inscription on Susan's mother's tombstone reads, "Susan Graham, wife of Col. W. Graham, Died in 1825. Aged 74 years." This would mean that mother and daughter both died in 1825 which, of course, is not impossible. However, the issue is further complicated by a paragraph in Lou Rogers's book *Tar Heel Women* stating that "years later, after his own wife died," Colonel Graham married Susan Twitty Miller, who then "died in

1825." The duplication of the names "Susan" and "William" Twitty have contributed much to the muddle.

Regardless of the confusion over dates, the story of Susan Twitty's bravery, passed down through the years, has inspired each generation in turn. On September 16, 1967, the Susan Twitty Chapter of the Children of the American Revolution presented a "dramatic episode" to celebrate the unveiling of a Graham's Fort Marker. Titled "Susan Twitty, Defender of Graham's Fort," the production starred local talent from Cleveland County. The historical marker, placed near the town of Grover, identifies the approximate location of Graham's Fort.

Standing on that spot, gazing at the magnificent foothills, one can almost hear the crack of a rifle and a defiant shout. A crow swoops low across the fields, cawing in the same raucous tone his ancestor used more than two hundred years ago. And each fall, the rich colors of autumn still set King's Mountain aflame.✤

ABIGAIL "AUNT ABBY" HOUSE

circa 1796–1881

Angel of Mercy

She certainly didn't look like an angel, at least not the angels seen in all the famous paintings. Those angels are young winged creatures in white gowns, their lovely faces aglow with heavenly joy. Any glow on Abby House's homely, sixty-five-year-old face was caused by wind and sun as she worked her small farm near Franklinton, North Carolina.

Abby was a somewhat stooped old woman who usually wore a faded homespun skirt, a long black cape, and a grim expression. Wings were not part of her ensemble. No one ever saw her wear white. Frequently seen clenching a corn cob pipe between her teeth, she would shake her cane at people in a threatening manner and whack them if they gave her trouble. At times, she carried two canes— one to maintain balance and the other to maintain control of the situation. She could fill the air with language that would make a soldier blush, and she often did.

Yet an angel she was, nonetheless, arriving in Virginia on a mission of mercy one bleak December day in 1862. Mouth set in a permanent frown, she stood atop Marye's Heights, just beyond the town of Fredericksburg. Behind her, hundreds of great, dark guns

ABIGAIL "AUNT ABBY" HOUSE

"Aunt Abby" House

NORTH CAROLINA DIVISION OF ARCHIVES AND HISTORY

rested at last, their deadly work temporarily finished. Soldiers in gray uniforms nodded to her as they passed, carrying the wounded into the house they had converted into a hospital.

At the bottom of the hill was a sunken road bordered by a stone wall. Crouching behind that wall, Confederate regiments had unloaded a steady barrage of shells, firing their muskets again and again on each successive wave of Union troops.

Abby's piercing black eyes gazed across the narrow plain between the road and the town of Fredericksburg. It was not the first time she had seen this monstrous War Between the States up close. During the past year and a half, she had nursed countless sick and wounded men in gray, taking others home to Franklin County to recover or to rest eternally in peace. But the view from Marye's Heights was a vision from hell far worse than anything she had seen before.

Bodies lay heaped on every square foot of ground, like the carcasses of cicadas that swarm in hoards across the land every thirteen years and perish all at once. In this scene, however, the stiffening shapes were the corpses of men—thousands of men. Blood-soaked and caked with mud, they slept a final sleep, their bodies far colder than December's frosty air. Time and time again they had surged forward toward the stone wall as their comrades fell to the right and left. Shrieking shells, roaring cannons, and voices crying out in terrified agony were the last sounds they heard as they died. Now, an eerie silence hung in the air, as thick as the stench of death.

As much as Abby House hated Yankees, the sight of the slaughtered men brought her no joy. She did, however, allow herself a moment of smug satisfaction. She leaned on her cane, her black cape flapping in the wind. So they thought they could just march straight to Richmond, did they? If so, they had been taught a valuable lesson.

But she had not come to gloat. She must look for Ned Sutton, her nephew. The Georgia regiment he belonged to could not account for him. They thought he might have been taken prisoner. Abby had to know. She had promised her nephews—all eight of them—that she would come and nurse them if they were sick or wounded and bring their bodies home if they died.

As she told noted North Carolina writer Mary Devereaux Bayard Clarke in an interview published in 1867, she was determined not to give up until she had "looked in the face of every man" on Fredericksburg's field of death. Clarke quoted Aunt Abby further: "Gin'ral Lee he gin' me a guard to go 'long o' me, for he was al'ers as good to me as he could be."

She searched among the dead for twelve days. At last, she located Ned.

> I know'd him when I got in ten steps of him; and says I to the man as was with me, "yonder's Ned." He was a leaning agin a fence, like as if he was a looking over it, and his hand was raised 'bout like he was a holding of his muskit with the butt end on it a resting on the ground when he was shot; his face was sorter turned over his shoulder, and it seemed to me he was a looking back, and a beckoning on me to come on keep my promise of burying him with his kin, and he had a sorter peaceful look as if he knowed I wouldn't forget it.

During the course of the war, Aunt Abby extended her loyalty and compassion to other members of the Franklinton community and to all Confederate soldiers. She was a common sight at the Raleigh–Gaston Railroad station, meeting cars filled with the wounded or taking the train herself to battlefields and hospitals. She never paid for a ride. And if the train didn't go all the way to her destination, she walked or hitchhiked as far as she had to.

Unable to read or write, Aunt Abby nevertheless knew what was needed and took action. What she lacked in formal education, she more than made up for with sheer grit and force of personality. Many was the time she gathered food, bedding, clothing, and other articles from her neighbors and carried the items herself to her men in gray, wherever they might be.

Abby, whose given name was Abigail, was the daughter of Green and Ann House of Granville and Franklin counties in North Carolina. Her date of birth was unknown, even by Abby herself. She claimed she was sixty-five years old when the Civil War began, which would mean she was born around 1796.

Much of the insight we have about Aunt Abby came from her encounter with Mary Devereaux Bayard Clarke, a remarkable woman in her own right. Born in 1827, Clarke was not only a prolific writer and poet herself, but she collected and preserved the writing of other North Carolina women as well. Her description of Abby House included a reference that must have made many of her readers chuckle. Abby was "a tall, Meg Merrilles looking woman," Clarke wrote, alluding to a poem penned by Englishman John Keats in the mid-1800s:

Old Meg she was a gipsy,
And liv'd upon the moors:
Her bed it was the brown heath turf,
And her house was out of doors. . .

Old Meg was brave as Margaret Queen*
And tall as Amazon:
An old red blanket cloak she wore;
A chip hat had she on.
God rest her aged bones somewhere—
She died full long agone!

* Queen Margaret of Scotland

Dr. R. H. Whitaker, a Methodist clergyman and editor of a temperance newspaper in Raleigh, met Abby House in her later years. He wrote of a conversation he had with her in 1877:

> "Aunt Abby House" was a native of Franklin County, born the latter part of the eighteenth century, according to her statement, being, as she once told me, "a right smart gal, enduring of the time of the war of 1812; big enough to have a sweetheart." That sweetheart, she said, went to the war, and the news came to her that he was sick at Norfolk, Va., and, she said, she walked every step of the way from Franklin County to Norfolk to see him, arriving there the day after he was buried. "O, yes," said she, "I was a right smart gal enduring of that war; but, I can't tell you exactly how old I am now."

Reports of Aunt Abby's courage have come from many sources, including her friend and neighbor Elizabeth Cooke. Mrs. Cooke presented a paper about Abby to the Joseph J. Davis Chapter of the United Daughters of the Confederacy in May of 1915, saying

> Was there a Franklin County boy sick, Aunt Abby would go to the front to nurse him? Did a family or sweetheart have a precious package for 'Johnny Reb,' Aunt Abby could be depended on to get through the lines and to safely deliver the cherished packet. Or was there trouble in obtaining a furlough, old Abby would start at once for headquarters and invariably return with some one or perhaps several pale and ragged convalescents to be nursed back to health by the loving hearts at home.

Aunt Abby's habit of traveling to headquarters illustrated one of her most endearing—or perhaps most disturbing—qualities, depending on your point of view. Rank meant nothing to her, and she was not intimidated by titles. If she wanted something, she went straight to the top, a technique she had learned through vast experience with lawyers and lawsuits. Clarke quoted her as stating:

> Now that's jest the way in the army, if you goes to the Captain, he sends you to the Major, and if you goes to the Major he sends you to the Curnel, so when I wanted anything I never wasted time on none 'er your understrappers—I went straight to President Davis or Gineral Lee, and I got it.

She frequently referred to Robert E. Lee as "Mause Bob" and to Jefferson Davis as "Jeff." Another person Abby felt perfectly comfortable "going straight to" was Zebulon Baird Vance, colonel in the Confederate army and wartime governor of North Carolina. Vance eventually became a United States senator after the War Between the States. One of Aunt Abby's most important encounters with him involved her nephew Marcellus. At Abby's request, Vance had written to Robert E. Lee, asking the General to grant Marcellus a thirty-day sick furlough with the promise that he would be sent back to the army when the furlough expired. About a month after Marcellus was supposed to have returned to his regiment, Abby paid a call on the governor. She stamped the snow off her boots, took a seat, and propped her feet up on the fender of his desk.

"Zeb," she said. "That boy can't go back to the army. He's got the consumption right now, and he'll die in less than a week if he goes back."

Aunt Abby was well aware that military hospitals were set up all over the region to meet the soldiers' needs, but she had lost faith in them long ago. Her nephew Dunc had been recovering nicely at the hospital in Petersburg after she spent several days there taking care of him. Shortly after returning to Franklinton, she received a letter telling her to hurry back if she wished to see him alive again. She arrived just before he passed away. She vowed, "The next one of my boys that gits down, I'm gwine ter bring him home if I has to go inter President Davis' bed-chamber to git the papers signed to do it."

The next time one of her nephews became ill, she set off for Richmond to see Davis. Fortunately, she did not have to accost him in his "bed chamber." Instead, she just slipped into his office when the door was left ajar. Once there, she criticized him harshly for the conditions in "his" hospitals.

"I'm doing my very best, Madam, I assure you," Davis said, drawing himself up.

"Well, if you's a doing of your best I should like to see some on it," said Abby. "For I be switched if all I've seed o' your hospitals ain't your level worst."

The quality of the army's health care services notwithstanding, Governor Vance expressed dismay that Marcellus was still languishing at home. He stressed to Abby that she must return him to General Lee immediately. If it had been at all possible for Aunt Abby's frown to deepen, it undoubtedly would have at that moment. Her shrewd black eyes narrowed. She demanded that Vance write another letter excusing Marcellus from service.

A few years after the incident, Mary Devereaux Bayard Clarke contacted Governor Vance for his version of what happened next. Vance replied with a detailed account, which Clarke quoted in her article "Aunt Abby, the Irrepressible":

> "Well, well" said I in despair, "who shall I write to?"
> "Write to Gin'ral Lee, I don't want no botherment with none of them officers."

I seized a pen and wrote about as follows:

"General: The ubiquitous, indefatigable and inevitable Mrs. House will hand you this. She asks me to say, that she says, that her nephew Marcellus, now at home thirty days over his leave, is still unable to return to duty. She says he has a most distressing "koff"... I fear that the air here is too far South for his lungs, and earnestly recommend that more salubrious atmosphere of the Rappahannock; and that when comfortably established there, he be made to take for his "koff" a compound of sulphur, saltpetre and charcoal, to be copiously administered by inhalation. I should be happy to learn the result of this prescription, and have the honor to be General, Your ob't serv't, Z.B. Vance."

Vance read the letter to Abby in a loud and pompous tone, and she was delighted with it. As he folded the missive, he warned her that many people in the army didn't like him, and some of them might make fun of the letter.

When Abby presented the letter to "Gin'ral Lee," he did seem to have a difficult time keeping a straight face while reading Vance's words. "I told him to dry that up," Abby told Vance later. "And he read it through very solemn and said it was a mighty smart letter."

Vance asked if Lee had excused Marcellus. Abby exclaimed "Lord bless you, honey, it never done a grain o' good."

Aunt Abby later told Clarke, "I only knows that Gin'ral Lee said it was a mighty smart letter, and seemed powerful sorry he could'nt let Marcellus stay at home that time cause he was afeard of the example."

Mrs. H. C. Taylor of Louisburg, North Carolina, offered another anecdote about Abby. She described an incident that took place in the spring of 1862, after the Seven Days Battle near Richmond. Her uncle, Richard P. Minga, tried to secure a pass through the lines to search for his son who had been wounded. To his dismay, he learned that the boy was in enemy hands. Taylor said:

> The disheartened father was more than a little surprised to hear a woman's voice say, "Mr. Minga, what in the world are you doing here?" He turned and found that the questioner was none other than Aunt Abby, on hand as usual, to do what she could for those who needed help. Abby told him to wait where he was and headed into the confusion, cane in hand. After a wait of several hours, he had practically given up hope . . . when he heard a commotion and looked up to see Aunt Abby approaching, followed by two Yankee stretcher bearers, carrying his wounded son between them.

Aunt Abby's love for her country—the Confederate States of America—was as fierce as the intense expression in her piercing black eyes. The idea that the Yankees might win the war caused her great pain and anger. She was on her way to General Lee's army when she heard of the evacuation of Richmond. At the same time, President Davis was scheduled to arrive in Greensboro. Mary Devereaux Bayard Clarke quoted Abby's recollection of that day.

> I couldn't work my way through to Gin'ral Lee 'afore he give up under that thar apple-tree, so I said to the boys: boys, I'm a gwine to jine President Davis since I can't git to Gin'ral Lee. . . . One of em told me to be sure when I got in sight of the inemy, to raise my right hand. "And now Aunt Abby," say he, "Don't you sass 'em none 'cause they ain't like us, and would as leave shoot an old woman as not." When I seed 'em, honey, I did raise my right

hand, but Lord bless your soul it was the heaviest lift ever
I tried, it seemed like I was made o' lead and had a hundred pound weight hung on the end o' my fingers. But I
knowed it wasn't my hand, but my heart that was so heavy.
. . . I walked through ten mile o' 'em, honey, and never
said nar'er a word. I thought I should 'er choked.

During the period immediately after the war, Abby's admira-
tion for Messrs. Vance, Lee, and Davis was matched only by her
loathing for William Woods Holden. Holden had become governor
of North Carolina in 1865, and Abby considered him a mere pup-
pet of the Yankees. His impeachment and removal from office in
1870 due to a corruption scandal undoubtedly caused the usually
grim line of her mouth to turn up just a bit at the ends.

Aunt Abby didn't have much patience with preachers and church
affairs during most of her life, but as she grew older, she mellowed
somewhat. In about 1875, according to Methodist minister R. H.
Whitaker, she made a profession of religion and joined the Methodist church. When Whitaker encountered her not long after, they
had a lively discussion about avoiding profanity and forgiving one's
enemies. She thought perhaps she could stop cursing—or certainly
curse less—but she did not think she would be able to forgive Bill
Holden "because he treated Zeb Vance so mean."

Later, when she heard that Holden had accepted the faith and
was going to be baptized into the church, she told the preacher to
have the water "biling" hot because old Bill Holden would surely
need it.

In 1877, Aunt Abby's beloved Zebulun returned to the
governor's seat. T. H. Pearce described the scene as Vance took the
oath of office: "Aunt Abby was standing on the platform taking in
everything with great interest. When the governor ended his part of
the ceremony by repeating the words, 'I will, so help me God,' Aunt

Abby was heard to say in a clearly audible voice, 'That you will honey, that you will.'"

As she aged and became more and more dependent upon charity, Abby found she was indeed able to forgive Bill Holden. He became a dear friend, frequently stopping by the little cottage where she spent her last days—a house paid for by a few Confederate soldiers who appreciated her kindness during the war. Neighbors reported that it was not at all unusual to see Governor Vance drawing a bucket of water from the well in her yard. R. H. Whitaker came by often as well. He recalled his last visit with her in *Whitaker's Reminiscences, Incidents and Anecdotes,* written in 1903:

> In the last days of Aunt Abby she was a quiet, gentle-minded old lady and seemed never happier than when in a prayer meeting . . . I went to see her a few days before her death, and as I was taking my leave of her I remarked that I was going away from the city for a few days. "Then," said she, "I'll tell you good-bye for good, for I won't be here when you come back, but will be with Minnie," alluding to my wife, who had died a little while before. And holding my hand for a moment she asked: "Do you want to send her any word?" I never saw her afterward.

In the spring of 1881, twenty years after the first shots of the Civil War were fired at Fort Sumter, Abby House passed away. She was buried in a grove of oak and pine trees about one quarter of a mile east of the railroad she had traveled so many times on her errands of mercy. Colonel Fred Olds of Raleigh placed a wooden marker over her grave which read "Aunt Abby House, Angel of Mercy to the Confederate Soldiers." When this marker rotted away it was replaced with a similar one by E. J. Cheatham of Franklinton. Cheatham kept a marker on her grave until his death in 1950.

For a long time after that, her grave was unmarked, its location known only to about a dozen people. Then, in 1974, T. H. Pearce reported that a stone patterned after the stones erected by the United Daughters of the Confederacy on Confederate graves across the state had been erected at Abby's grave. P. H. Cheatham, owner of the land on which Abby was buried, helped put the marker in place. Pearce wrote: "It certainly won't be seen by many, and it might even seem a useless gesture to some, but thanks to people like J. F. McLeod and others who helped, Aunt Abby finally has a marker. We think she deserves it."

The words Zeb Vance used to describe Abby House to General Lee are worth repeating. He called her "ubiquitous," which means existing or being everywhere at the same time; "indefatigable," meaning untiring; and "inevitable," which means incapable of being avoided. Interestingly enough, those same words could be used to describe certain celestial beings called angels.✤

HARRIET ANN JACOBS
1813–1897

Hideaway Slave

The year Harriet Ann Jacobs turned twenty-two, the United States turned fifty-nine. Samuel Morse invented the telegraph. Texas seceded from Mexico. The Liberty Bell cracked while tolling the death of Chief Justice John Marshall.

That same year, Harriet Jacobs climbed up into a tiny crawlspace above a shed. A trap door closed behind her with a click. Lying on her back and extending her arms, Harriet could almost touch the highest point of the sharply sloping roof. She could not sit up. Every time she turned over, she bumped the roof. The space was just slightly larger than a coffin, measuring nine feet long and seven feet wide.

As time passed, Harriet's eyes grew accustomed to the dim lighting in her garret. If she lay on her stomach or side, she could actually read or sew. Food was handed to her through the trap door. At night, when there was less danger of discovery, her grandmother, aunt, or uncle would talk briefly with her at the opening.

On summer days, the heat was nearly unbearable, and hundreds of little red insects tormented Harriet. During cold spells, she shivered inside a blanket, chilled to the bone. Winters were rela-

NORTH CAROLINA DIVISION OF ARCHIVES AND HISTORY

Harriet Ann Jacobs

tively short and mild where she lived, but the temperature could still dip below freezing at night.

Occasionally, during daylight hours, Harriet squinted through a tiny hole she had drilled in her wall, hoping to catch a glimpse of her two children. They had not been told where she was. Once in a very great while, under cover of darkness, she ventured down into the storeroom below her crawlspace. There she tried to relieve the stiffness and numbness in her limbs by moving about. As fall faded into winter and winter blossomed into spring, she wondered how much longer she could tolerate such narrow confinement. She endured it for seven years.

Harriet Ann Jacobs was born in 1813 in Edenton, North Carolina, a picturesque town at the head of the Albemarle Sound. The first official capital of the colony, Edenton's roots reached deep into the soil of American history. Here the Chowanoc Indians settled, making the mighty Chowan River their major highway and reaping its rich bounty of fish. Here on the peninsula formed by Pembroke and Queen Anne's Creeks, adventurers from Jamestown founded a community in 1658. Before long, the vast Atlantic Ocean brought deep-sea ships, whalers, and rum boats to dock in Edenton Bay. Their masts and riggings rose like intricate latticework against the horizon.

Mother England considered Edenton a "problem child," for it seemed to be continuously in revolt against the Crown. In 1774, a group of more than fifty Edenton women pledged to boycott all products from England "until such time that all acts which tend to enslave our Native country shall be repealed." Joseph Hewes, a prominent Edenton citizen, was one of three men from North Carolina to sign the Declaration of Independence in 1776.

In those days, the fresh air of freedom mingled with the salty ocean breeze, creating a new, invigorating climate. Terms like "inalienable rights" and phrases like "all men are created equal" stirred the souls of every person who lived in America. Those who were slaves eagerly anticipated release not only from the tyranny of King George but from the restrictions imposed by their colonial masters. Many looked forward to returning to Africa, their homeland.

But they were doomed to disappointment. It seemed not everyone in the new nation was considered eligible for "life, liberty, and the pursuit of happiness." By the second decade of the 1800s, the "land of the free" contained 1.2 million slaves. Eli Whitney's cotton gin had given the southern states a new lease on life, and slave labor was more important than ever.

During this time, kidnapping of free African-Americans was widespread. The Fugitive Slave Act of 1793 allowed any white person to claim a black person as a fugitive, unless another white person testified otherwise. In a town famous for its opposition to enslavement, Harriet Ann Jacobs learned firsthand the effects of that ancient institution on the human spirit.

"I was born and reared in Slavery," she wrote in the preface to her book *Incidents in the Life of a Slave Girl*, published in 1861. "And I remained in a Slave State twenty-seven years."

In writing a narrative of her life, Harriet Jacobs hoped to "arouse the women of the North to a realizing sense of the condition of two millions of women at the South, still in bondage, suffering what I suffered, and most of them far worse."

According to James Davis in *The Heritage of Blacks in North Carolina*, Harriet's grandmother Molly was emancipated during the American Revolution but was captured by American forces while traveling from British-occupied South Carolina to Florida. She was sold back into slavery as a prize of war. Molly's daughter Delilah and her husband, Daniel Jacobs, had two children, Harriet and John.

When Harriet was six, her mother passed away, and Harriet was surprised to learn that she and her four-year-old brother were not people, but property. They belonged to their mother's mistress.

Fortunately, the mistress treated Delilah's children well. She taught Harriet to sew, shared stories with her from the Bible, and even taught her how to read and spell. In 1825, however, she became very sick and died. Brokenhearted at the loss of yet another loved one, twelve-year-old Harriet was immediately jolted by an additional shock: her mistress had willed her to her sister's child, age five. Later, as an adult, Harriet recalled her feelings:

> My mistress had taught me the precepts of God's Word: "Thou shalt love thy neighbor as thyself." "Whatsoever ye would that men should do unto you, do ye even so unto them." But I was her slave, and I supposed she did not recognize me as her neighbor. I would give much to blot out from my memory that one great wrong. As a child, I loved my mistress; and, looking back on the happy days I spent with her, I try to think with less bitterness of this act of injustice.

In *Incidents in the Life of a Slave Girl*, Harriet used fictitious names for everyone she wrote about, including herself, because she "deemed it kind and considerate toward others to pursue this course." She referred to her new master and mistress, the parents of the five-year-old, as "Dr. and Mrs. Flint." In calling them flint—a hard, gray stone—she clearly revealed her opinion of their level of compassion.

Harriet had been a member of the Flint household less than a year when her father passed away. Not long after that, her grandmother's mistress died, granting Molly her freedom. In spite of the mistress's directive regarding her slave, Dr. Flint, executor of the estate, planned to sell her privately. To thwart his efforts, Molly marched up onto the block on auction day. Members of the community who knew and respected her were appalled and refused to bid on her. Finally, she was purchased for fifty dollars by her mistress's elderly sister, who publicly set her free.

As time went on, Harriet witnessed many other indications that Dr. Flint lacked the milk of human kindness. Although she herself was spared the beatings, brandings, mutilations, and other cruelties inflicted upon some of the slaves, she learned that no matter what form abuse takes, it is always painful. In *Incidents in the Life of a Slave Girl*, she wrote: "I now entered on my fifteenth year—a sad epoch in the life of a slave girl. My master began to whisper foul words in my ear. Young as I was, I could not remain ignorant of their import. . . . He told me I was his property; that I must be subject to his will in all things."

Harriet resisted Flint's advances, but his pursuit was relentless.

"In desperation I told him that I must and would apply to my grandmother for protection," she wrote. "He threatened me with death, and worse than death, if I made any complaint to her."

When a free-born African-American man fell in love with Harriet and offered to buy her, Dr. Flint denied the request. Harriet knew then that she would never be allowed to pledge herself to someone she loved and live a normal married life.

When Mrs. Flint demanded that Harriet tell her everything that had taken place between her and Dr. Flint, Harriet replied honestly, hoping the mistress would protect her from further abuse. Instead, Mrs. Flint refused to believe Harriet's testimony that nothing had actually happened. Furious, she began to jealously monitor Harriet's every move. This helped keep Dr. Flint in check but also caused Harriet to fear for her safety.

Molly, knowing her granddaughter was miserable, offered to buy her. Dr. Flint refused, stating that Harriet was his daughter's property, and he did not have the right to sell her.

The harassment continued. Before long, Flint told Harriet he was having a cottage built about four miles from town. He promised that if she would live there and do his bidding, she would be treated well. She refused the offer. His suggestion went against every law of decency her family had taught her. In addition, she did not trust Flint to keep his word. Later, she wrote: "I knew that as soon as a new fancy took him, his victims were sold far off to get rid of them; especially if they had children. . . . He never allowed his offspring by slaves to remain long in sight of himself and his wife."

In spite of Harriet's refusal, Flint proceeded to build the cottage. While it was under construction, Harriet found herself courted by a compassionate white man who knew her grandmother. She couldn't help wondering if a relationship with Mr. Sands, as she referred to him in her book, might be a way out of Flint's clutches. If she became pregnant, perhaps the doctor would be angry enough to sell her and the baby. She felt certain that under the circumstances, Mr. Sands, an "educated and eloquent gentleman," would buy them and set them free. Since Mr. Sands did not have a wife, Harriet reasoned, she would not be causing another woman pain by her actions. In addition, as she later wrote: "There is something akin to freedom in having a lover who has no control over you, except that which he gains by kindness and attachment."

Harriet was ashamed of entering into a sexual relationship with Mr. Sands, but she was desperate. In 1829, she gave birth to his son, naming him Joseph. Dr. Flint was furious, but instead of selling Harriet and her child, he vowed they would be his slaves forever. She wrote: "Sometimes, when my master found that I still refused to accept what he called his kind offers, he would threaten to sell my child. 'Perhaps that will humble you,' said he. His threat lacerated my heart. I knew the law gave him power to fulfil it."

At the age of nineteen, Harriet bore Mr. Sands's second child, Louisa Matilda. This further enraged Dr. Flint, and he swore he would make her suffer for it.

Not long after, he came up with another proposition: If she

discontinued all communication with the children's father and brought them to live with her in the cottage Flint had built, he would free all three of them. If she declined, they would all be sent to labor on his son's plantation. Joseph would be put to work and then sold. Louisa would be raised for the purpose of selling as well. He announced that Harriet had one week to consider the offer. Harriet needed less than one minute. Her refusal was immediate and emphatic. Flint stormed out.

"My master had power and law on his side," Harriet wrote. "I had a determined will. There is might in each."

Harriet went to work at the younger Flint's plantation. When she overheard Dr. Flint telling his son to bring her children there to be "broken in," she knew she had to take action. She ran away and concealed herself at a friend's house, hoping Flint would give up searching for her within a few weeks. As soon as she was discovered missing, he posted a notice:

> $300 REWARD! Ran away from the subscriber, an in-telligent, bright, mulatto girl . . . 21 years of age. Five feet four inches high. Dark eyes, and black hair inclined to curl; but it can be made straight. Has a decayed spot on a front tooth. She can read and write, and in all probability will try to get to the Free States.

Harriet hid for a time at the home of a sympathetic white woman in the community. Flint had Harriet's children, her brother, John, and her aunt jailed to try to force them to tell where she was (they didn't know). Thinking she might have escaped to New York, he traveled there to look for her. Two months passed.

In the meantime, Mr. Sands and some of Harriet's other friends arranged to have a slave trader buy John, Joseph, and Louisa from Flint. After giving the matter some thought, he agreed, and the transaction went through. The three slaves now belonged to Sands, who returned the children to their grandmother. When Flint learned what had happened, he told Molly that he would never give up searching for Harriet. Harriet knew she would have to find another hiding place.

In *Incidents in the Life of a Slave Girl*, she wrote:

> A small shed had been added to my grandmother's house years ago. Some boards were laid across the joists at the top, and between these boards and the roof was a very small garret, never occupied by any thing but rats and mice. . . . There was no admission for either light or air

In 1835, at the age of twenty-two, Harriet Ann Jacobs crawled into the tomblike space above Molly's storeroom. Christmas came and went, bringing mixed emotions. Harriet could hear her children's voices and occasionally see their faces, but she could not speak to them or let them know of her presence. She had to find contentment in the belief that her disappearance had liberated them from Dr. Flint's power.

During her stay in Molly's garret, Harriet wrote letters and had friends mail them from New York, Boston, and Canada. After a long while, Flint seemed resigned to the idea that she had escaped to the North. Toward the end of her fifth year in hiding, Harriet and Molly decided it was safe for Harriet to come down into the storeroom more often. They feared she would be crippled for life if she did not get more exercise.

That same year, Harriet's brother escaped while on a trip to Washington with Mr. Sands. Soon after that, Dr. Flint was heard boasting that Harriet's children still belonged to his daughter, and that the sales contract he had signed was not legally binding. Mr. Sands suggested to Molly that Louisa be sent to live with one of his relatives in New York. Sick at heart but determined to do what was best for Louisa, Harriet agreed with the plan. Sands also said that Joseph could move North whenever Harriet's uncle was ready to go with him.

One morning in 1842, seven years after Harriet had first crawled into her tiny garret, freedom rose on the horizon. A friend of Harriet's had made secret arrangements for her to travel to the Free States by ship. Although terrified that her granddaughter might be captured and horribly punished, Molly sent Harriet away with her blessing. After sunset that night, Harriet boarded the vessel that would take her to a new life. Later, she wrote:

> I shall never forget that night. The balmy air of spring was so refreshing! And how shall I describe my sensations when we were fairly sailing on Chesapeake Bay? O, the beautiful sunshine! The exhilarating breeze! and I could enjoy them without fear or restraint. I had never realized what grand things air and sunlight are till I had been deprived of them.

Not long after arriving in Philadelphia, Harriet learned that escaping to the North did not guarantee total freedom and equality with the white race. To her surprise, she discovered that African-Americans were not allowed to ride in the first-class train car.

"This was the first chill to my enthusiasm about the Free States," she wrote. "Colored people were allowed to ride in a filthy box, behind white people, at the south, but there they were not required to pay for the privilege. It made me sad to find how the north aped the customs of slavery."

Still, in her new home, there seemed to be more reasons to hope for a better future. Reunited with her daughter and brother, Harriet soon celebrated her son's arrival as well. The winter of 1844–

1845 was the first time Harriet and her children had been together since Harriet went into hiding. Two years passed in relative peace, with Harriet working diligently for her own support and the education of her children.

Even in the midst of her newfound relief and joy, Harriet could never forget that she was a hunted woman. She worried that someone would recognize her on the street. On several occasions, she was forced to flee from New York upon being warned that Dr. Flint was coming to get her. In each case, a sympathetic and generous employer aided her in her flight. Even after Flint died, his daughter attempted to claim her "property." The Fugitive Slave Act of 1850 emboldened her in her efforts.

Appalled by the situation, Harriet's employer hired a man to enter into negotiations with Flint's daughter and her husband. In the end, Harriet was purchased for three hundred dollars. Her victory was bittersweet. In *Incidents in the Life of a Slave Girl*, she wrote:

> So I was sold at last! A human being sold in the free city of New York! The bill of sale is on record, and future generations will learn from it that women were articles of traffic in New York, late in the nineteenth century of the Christian religion. . . . I well know the value of that bit of paper; but much as I love freedom, I do not like to look upon it. I am deeply grateful to the generous friend who procured it, but I despise the miscreant who demanded payment for what never rightfully belonged to him or his.

Harriet's grandmother lived long enough to hear of her granddaughter's liberation but died soon after, in 1853.

Urged by Amy Post, a highly respected member of the Society of Friends (Quakers) in the State of New York, Harriet undertook to write a narrative of her experiences. Although the former slave was reluctant to be thrust into the public eye, Post convinced her that an account such as hers would surely "arouse people to a more earnest work for the disinthralment of millions still remaining in that soul-crushing condition" known as slavery.

Incidents in the Life of a Slave Girl was published in 1861. That same year, Confederate soldiers fired on Fort Sumter, igniting the first flames of the Civil War. During the war, Harriet used her celebrity to help raise money for African-American refugees. After the war, she spent her time helping freed slaves by distributing relief supplies, teaching, and providing health care.

The year Harriet Ann Jacobs turned fifty-four, the United States turned ninety-one. African-American human rights leader Frederick Douglass issued his "Appeal to Congress for Impartial Suffrage." Wilbur Wright, co-inventor of the first airplane, was born. The United States purchased Alaska from Russia for $7.2 million.

That year, Harriet Ann Jacobs returned to Edenton. In April, she wrote a letter to Ednah Dow Cheney, a Boston abolitionist:

> I am sitting under the old roof twelve feet from the spot where I suffered all the crushing weight of slavery. Thank God the bitter cup is drained of its last dreg. . . . I have hunted up all the old people, done what I could for them. I love to work for these old people. Many of them I have known from Childhood. . . . The white members of the Baptist Church invited the colored members to their Church, to help them sing and pray. I assure you they have done it with a will . . . my love to Miss Daisy [Cheney's daughter]. I send her some Jassmine blossoms. Tell her they bear the fragrance of freedom.✤

AUTHOR'S NOTE: The master and his family described in Jacobs's book were very real people and well known in their community. However, my purpose in including this chapter is not to cast blame on those individuals, who behaved in much the same way as many of their peers, but to illustrate the remarkable courage and determination of Miss Jacobs. For that reason, I have chosen to use the fictional names she used for her master and his family in her original work. According to James Davis in his article for Volume I of *The Heritage of Blacks in North Carolina*: "For a century the authorship of her book was in doubt. A new edition, annotated and edited by Jean Pagan Yellin, was published in 1987 by Harvard University Press, showing Harriet Ann Jacobs as the true author of *Incidents in the Life of a Slave Girl, Written by Herself*."

CORNELIA PHILLIPS SPENCER

1825–1908

Patron Saint of Chapel Hill

Horses in the library? Scalawags at the lecterns? Carpetbaggers guiding the future of North Carolina's brightest, most promising young men?

Cornelia Phillips Spencer's reaction quickly swung from disbelief to dismay to disgust. In her forty-four years of life she had weathered her share of disasters, but this latest development was simply intolerable. So much had been ruined during the War Between the States, it was painful to watch as insult was added to injury under the misnomer "Reconstruction."

It was bad enough that Yankee troops had trampled, burned, and torn apart nearly everything the South held dear. The war was over, yet the assault continued. Union military forces occupied Cornelia's beloved village of Chapel Hill. They seemed to have little respect for the birthplace of America's first state college—the University of North Carolina—built there in 1795. For three-quarters of a century the school had stood proudly on a hill originally called New Hope Chapel, overlooking rich acres of flat land that spread out from its base like an ocean.

Cornelia Phillips Spencer

NORTH CAROLINA DIVISION OF ARCHIVES AND HISTORY

To Cornelia's alarm, in the wake of the war's destruction, newly-elected governor William W. Holden abruptly dismissed the president and faculty of the university, stating, "It's time to clean out the rickety old concern." The word spread that federal soldiers were stabling their horses in the basement of the school's library.

"It's a terribly bitter thing for all respectable people in the State," Cornelia wrote in a diary entry dated "Spring, 1868."

To Cornelia, "the Hill" was home. She had been born in New York, but in 1826, when she was one year old, her family moved to North Carolina. At that time, Chapel Hill was, in her words, "the remotest town of the quietest county of the most backward old State in the Union."

Her father, James Phillips, was an Englishman who served as the university's chair of mathematics. Her mother, Judith Vermeule, was a bright, cultured woman of Dutch descent. From earliest childhood, Cornelia was hungry to learn. Unfortunately, suitable reading material was sometimes difficult to find. Each time her mother took her shopping, Cornelia slipped behind a platform at the store to read *Journal of a Residence in America* by London actress Fanny Kemble, wife of a Georgia plantation owner. She continued the practice until she had finished both volumes of the book.

Cornelia and her two brothers, Charles and Samuel, grew up on the campus, surrounded by deep green forests and flowers of every imaginable name and hue. Here, they were also treated to the advantages of an academic setting. At seventeen, Cornelia became frustrated with her father's efforts to impart his enthusiasm for science and mathematics. As she was often known to do, she committed her thoughts to poetry, asking:

Does science bring you nearer God?
Or free your soul from all alarm?

If not, this deep research, how vain!
How vain such useless lore to crave,
That rescues not from toil and pain,
Nor saves one votary from the grave.

Charles and Samuel Phillips both earned degrees from UNC. Charles became a professor of applied mathematics at the college, and Samuel became a lawyer and served as solicitor general of the United States for twelve years. Because Cornelia was female, she was not allowed to enroll at UNC. This did not prevent her, however, from reading and learning as much as possible on her own.

Nothing escaped her thirsty mind. She had an exceptional memory and could recite pages of poetry and whole chapters of novels. In later life, she was often described as a perfectly balanced blend of intuition and intellect.

The Civil War and its aftermath deeply offended Cornelia's sensibilities. Her dear university was closed in 1868, then reopened in 1869 under new leadership. To Cornelia's disgust, the new president, Solomon Pool, and his staff had been appointed based on political affiliation, not on their qualifications as administrators or teachers. They were nothing more than carpetbaggers and scalawags—corrupt opportunists who took advantage of the South's weakened condition to line their own pockets.

Cornelia herself was not at her strongest. In 1861, she had returned to Chapel Hill from Alabama, where she had been living with her husband James Spencer, a University of North Carolina graduate. The couple had been married just four years when James succumbed to a mysterious illness and passed away. To make matters worse, Cornelia began to realize that she was losing her hearing. She brought her young daughter, June, home to the oak and fig trees and gardens of brilliant blossoms so dear to her own childhood.

That same year, shots were fired on Fort Sumter. The "land of the free and the home of the brave" was rent asunder. In 1865, weary and deeply discouraged, Cornelia Spencer wrote:

> I have come to the conclusion that the great American people are a failure. I see in these days so much meanness, injustice, servility, malignity, narrow-minded bigotry, and selfishness, envy, hatred and malice, both north and south, that I cannot help thinking that we are a radically mean people.

When the university's honorable, dedicated president and faculty were dismissed and replaced with disreputable miscreants, Cornelia fell deeper into despair. "I am so worried and tormented as it were out of my very life!" she wrote in her diary. "How I long to get up and flee away out of it all." She had just about decided to leave Chapel Hill when she began to receive encouraging messages from her friends. One note was from Zebulon Baird Vance, UNC alumnus and governor of the state during the war. He wrote:

> We should not desert her [North Carolina] in the day of her humiliation. I love her the more because of her sorrows and degradation. I should be greatly pleased to hear that the way has been opened for you to remain here and abet us in watching for the better day whose dawning we do not doubt.

His words re-energized Cornelia's fighting spirit. She set aside her personal sorrows and prepared for battle against the scoundrels who had commandeered the college. Louis R. Wilson, in his introduction to *Selected Papers of Cornelia Spencer*, wrote: "[This woman] alone, and armed only with her pen, formulated a plan of action and determinedly stuck to it."

Cornelia's attack against President Pool and his colleagues was four-pronged. Her "Pen and Ink Sketches of the University," published in the *Raleigh Sentinel,* were designed to remind North Carolinians of the college's exemplary performance over the past seven decades. Faced with this constant reminder of what the school had been as recently as a year ago, readers couldn't help seeing the Pool administration as a poor, even fraudulent, substitute.

Cornelia's second method of attack was to write letters to the alumni and friends of the university, urging them to take action. She also secured the cooperation of the editors of several leading papers in the state. The *Raleigh Sentinel* and *Wilmington Journal* both published strong and frequent editorials on the disgraceful situation in Chapel Hill. Finally, Cornelia contributed countless articles to the press, some under her own name and others under pseudonyms. She scorched the usurpers to the academic throne with her fiery wit, labeling them "incomparable incapables."

Cornelia succeeded in pulling the plug on Pool, and, largely due to her efforts, his entire regime went rapidly down the drain. In March of 1869, in a letter to Mrs. D. L. Swain, wife of the college's former president, she wrote: "The University opened on the third. No students have appeared, or can be detected even with the aid of a magnifying glass. I am divided between exultation that it is so, and sorrow for the poor village, so utterly dependent on the college for its living."

On February 8, 1871, in an editorial for the *North Carolina Presbyterian,* she observed acerbically:

Gov. Holden's University opened its fifth session on the 14th with an "average attendance" of four students. It was then postponed to the 29th, at which time there were two students. Being thus whittled down to the little end of nothing, it is reported that the Faculty threaten to "resign." By all means.

The carpetbaggers were sent packing, and the university closed its doors for the second time since the end of the war.

Now, Cornelia Spencer geared up for a new crusade—her own version of Reconstruction. As reported a century later in a tribute that appeared in the *Durham Morning Herald*: "Mrs. Spencer continued to write. Her new theme was 'Come Back.' She appealed to North Carolina to re-open the university. Her campaign continued, in newspapers and in letters to prominent North Carolina people."

Months passed. Gradually, the once-bustling, vital college town became "The Deserted Village of the South." Weeds grew up, threatening to choke the azaleas, violets, and trillium that graced the wooded campus. Buildings fell into disrepair. In 1873, in the *Raleigh Sentinel*, Cornelia wrote: "Chapel Hill remains like a city broken down and without walls." She continued by saying that it was the duty of North Carolinians to forgive Governor Holden, "the man whose mistaken notions of his duty for several years so galled their feelings and outraged their liberties." However, she found it nearly impossible to do her share "as a christian citizen towards this amnesty" when she saw what had become of "the once prosperous village."

Nevertheless, Cornelia persisted, brandishing her pen to direct supporters much like an orchestra conductor wields a baton. Numerous alumni and friends of the college, many of whom had become prominent and influential over the years, tuned their instruments and rallied to her call. A staunch Presbyterian, Cornelia worked, prayed, and worked some more for the cause. Yet in mid-December of 1874, she reported "I hear of no plan for [the University's] relief and no prospect."

Just a few weeks into the new year, however, a very different message appeared from Cornelia in the *North Carolina Presbyterian*:

> I received a letter today from a gentleman, which spoke of the restoration of the University as something to be looked for now, not far off. I cannot write of it without tears swelling—I cannot speak of it without a sob. Since reading that letter I have been sitting with my head in my hands, picturing these Halls thrown open, these buildings tenanted, these groves once more vocal, these decaying residences repaired, this deserted village again prosperous and populous.

Finally, on March 20, 1875—the day she turned fifty years old—Cornelia received a telegram. The North Carolina General Assembly had voted in a new board of trustees for the university. The hallowed halls of Chapel Hill would once again echo with the lively conversation of students and teachers. No birthday gift could have pleased her more.

Her emotions high, she gathered a few friends and marched to the old South building. Up the stairs she climbed, three floors, then up further still into the belfry. For thirty minutes—some say an hour—Cornelia Spencer rang the bell. Her partial deafness forgotten, she rejoiced as the sound reverberated all around her, turning the air itself into the most melodious instrument of her vast orchestra.

In September of 1875, she helped weave the garlands that decorated the chapel at the re-opening of the university. Her voice joined with those of her dear friends as they sang a hymn she had written for the occasion. On a hot, sunny day in early June 1876, she thrilled to the sight of the crowded chapel, with "750 fans in motion at once" during commencement exercises.

Amazingly, Cornelia Spencer's impact on the state of North Carolina was accomplished without her ever making a public appearance. She was not a speaker or gladhander, riding through town on a wagon and waving at the crowd. Described as "a majestic woman, strong and noble as a Hebrew prophetess," "handsome, much above the usual size, with an imposing figure . . . and large, lustrous eyes," she no doubt could have influenced decisions by her mere presence. Instead, she spent most of her life in a "narrow segment of street, containing not more than seven or eight houses." She sculpted her world with the point of her pen—literally. There was no such thing as a typewriter in her day.

Her sharp intellect impressed everyone who met her. When someone described her as the smartest woman in North Carolina, Zeb Vance rejoined: "And the smartest man, too."

Although exceedingly charitable, Cornelia had strong opinions on nearly every subject, and did not hesitate to voice them. She had nothing but scorn for women who would don a split skirt and pedal about town on a bicycle. Women could and should expand their roles in society, she put forth, but certain areas were simply inappropriate. She considered a woman to be after "Forbidden Fruit" if she tried "to hold the reins of civil government, to legislate, to be an 'orator,' to ascend the pulpit and usurp its duties, to sit on the Bench and give judgment."

About women's rights, she observed: "Reform is a good thing when it does not come all at once, and knows when to stop." By the same token, she disputed the idea that women's rights should be sharply curtailed in order to prevent them from going too far.

"It is not always true that if you give an inch an ell will be taken," she wrote. "But if you refuse an inch when the inch is clearly due, the ell is almost sure to be seized in the rumpus that follows." An "ell" is a unit of length measuring forty-five inches.

On some occasions, Cornelia proved herself more open-minded than most. As devoted as she was to the Confederacy, she refused to denounce the marriage of Governor Swain's daughter Eleanor to General Smith B. Atkins of Illinois. Atkins had met Ellie Swain when he occupied the town with his soldiers following the war. The wedding "rocked Chapel Hill to its foundations," reported *Chapel Hill Weekly*. Cornelia, however, defended Ellie Swain's choice and attended the ceremony, even though it gave the governor and his wife "as much uneasiness as anything short of a death in the family could have done."

Among Cornelia's numerous writings was a book called *The Last Ninety Days of the War*, published in 1866. In its pages, she presented a vivid picture of the final three months of the catastrophe that plagued the nation for five long years. She also penned *First Steps in North Carolina History*, a small volume quickly put to use in the public schools. Her sketches "Old Days in Chapel Hill" appeared in serial form in the *University Magazine*. In 1953, a collection of her work was published by the University of North Carolina Press as *Selected Papers of Cornelia Phillips Spencer*.

Had Cornelia's only gift been her ability to communicate and convince through the written word, she would have been remarkable enough. As it was, listing areas where she did not excel would probably take less time than cataloguing her many talents. She was a mother, poet (or "occasional versifier," as she put it), historian, journalist, painter, and environmentalist. She played the piano, too.

Guided by a deep religious faith, she never hesitated to help the downtrodden. George T. Winston, president of the University of North Carolina from 1891 to 1896, wrote:

Nobody was a stranger to her charity; nobody was too humble nor too depraved for her sympathy and help.

Although herself of limited means, she was a giver of charity to the poor; of original poems or dainty needle work; of pretty painted souvenirs to friends and neighbors; of good words and good cheer to everybody; of hospitality to all who entered her doors.

Mrs. Winston described Cornelia Spencer's essential character in an article for the *News and Observer*:

Mrs. Spencer was a ministering angel to needy and suffering neighbors, both white and black, rich and poor, in time of sickness her help never failed. . . . It was as a neighbor and a friend, as a housekeeper, a giver of bread to the needy, a lover of the wild woods, a friend of everybody and everything in Chapel Hill and North Carolina that I knew Mrs. Spencer best and remember her most vividly.

Cornelia did indeed love "the wild woods." She wrote at length and in great detail about the beauty of the local flora. In one essay, she described the trees and flowers of spring as if they were participants in a fashion show.

In the first of our season the willows and the wheat fields, and the peach trees had it all their own way, and pale green and pink were your only wear, though along the brook sides the alders were sturdily independent, and preferred to hang out a tawny tassel shot with gold dust. The dog-tooth violets, too appeared to think the variable and uncertain season demanded something less delicate than pink—and such tender green. So they opened heavy satin leaves of tea-green dappled with brown, and striped their yellow bells with the same shade, declaring they could not face the winds of March unless they were well wrapped up with colors that would wear.

A staunch champion for public schools, Cornelia Spencer had an especially keen interest in the education of women. In 1877, a State Normal and Industrial College for Women was created, the first of its kind in America. For Cornelia, the school represented two of her ideals: higher education opportunities for women and the long-overdue training of public school teachers. Her contributions and support were acknowledged by placing her name on buildings at UNC and the Normal and Industrial College, eventually renamed "Woman's College."

In the 1880s, Cornelia's daughter, Julia (called "June"), married James Lee Love, a distinguished member of UNC's Class of 1884 who subsequently joined the faculty. A few years later, he took a position at Harvard, and he and June moved to Massachusetts. It was in their Cambridge home that Cornelia, by then completely deaf, lived the last decade of her life. Although she missed Chapel Hill, she delighted in Harvard's library and in the familiarity of the college setting. In a journal she kept from 1882 to 1904, she wrote: "July 16th, 1904 Cornelia [her granddaughter, Cornelia Love] and I to Harvard Lib. once more. A great peaceful pleasure to walk through that campus."

In 1895, after she had moved into her daughter's home, she became the first woman to receive the University of North Carolina's highest honorary degree: Doctor of Laws. Women were first admitted to the university in 1897. However, admittance was permitted only for bona fide residents of Chapel Hill in graduate courses or as upper level transfers. It was 1917 before women were admitted to the college as freshmen.

In her last journal entry, dated August of 1904, Cornelia

Spencer wrote: "I lay the book aside with gratitude to the Disposer of my life for the protection he has given me the blessings and enjoyments, and the time for preparation. The end of a long life is now not far off."

Cornelia Phillips Spencer died in Cambridge in March of 1908, just before her eighty-third birthday. It was reported that she was holding a picture of the university campus in her hand when she passed away. Her body was returned to Chapel Hill for burial in the village cemetery. As a tribute to her memory, all classes were suspended, and the college bell in the South building—the bell Cornelia had rung to announce the re-opening of the University in 1875— tolled in slow reverence.

Honors continued to be bestowed on this remarkable woman long after she died. In the spring of 1943, the *"Cornelia Phillips Spencer,"* a victory merchant ship, was launched at Wilmington, North Carolina. That same year, Cornelia's son-in-law, James Lee Love, established the Cornelia P. Spencer Alumni Fund by donating one thousand shares of common stock in the Burlington Mills Corporation.

Today, the University of North Carolina at Chapel Hill is stronger than ever. In 1997, more than twenty-four thousand students were enrolled. Women account for nearly fifty-nine percent of the total student enrollment and are represented in every academic field. In 1927, Sallie B. Marks became the first woman to join the regular faculty as assistant professor of elementary education. The percentage of women among faculty rose from sixteen percent in 1977 to over thirty-two percent in 1997. (Cornelia would have approved. She considered Woman a natural teacher, stating: "She does it insensibly every day of her life, whether of set purpose in a schoolroom or not.")

As for the rumor about Yankee horses being stabled in the library during Reconstruction, the UNC Internet website reports:

"A persistent but unsubstantiated campus legend has it that the horses of the Michigan Ninth Cavalry were stabled in the library after the Civil War. This stimulated the story that, since then, Michigan horses have been known for their intelligence and Carolina students for their horse sense." ❧

EMELINE JAMISON PIGOTT

1836–1919

Confederate Spy

Emeline Pigott's eyes met those of the two Northern men who stood before her.

"Write it down," she said. "I must have it in writing."

She looked around nervously. There were many strangers in Beaufort, North Carolina, these days. The Federals had taken over the town nearly two years ago—in the spring of 1862. Emeline never knew who might be lurking nearby. She had heard rumors that the Yankees suspected her of being a spy. If she were caught, she would be killed, and she wasn't about to let that happen.

These two men from the North were no more than despicable profiteers, but Emeline had decided to trust them. On several occasions, they had helped her smuggle food, clothing, mail, and medicine through the lines to her dear Southern soldiers. They were now offering her valuable information about Unionist plans that would mean a great deal to General Lee.

One of the men thrust a piece of paper into her hand. With a quick glance in all directions, Emeline nodded her thanks, turned, and walked briskly away, the hem of her hoopskirt floating about her ankles. As a young girl, she had hated the uncomfortable cloth-

Emeline Jamison Pigott

NORTH CAROLINA DIVISION OF ARCHIVES AND HISTORY

ing styles of her day. As a twenty-eight-year-old woman trying to conceal provisions for an army, she found the billowing garments quite useful. With a few large pins strategically placed under her petticoats, she became a human supply train. On certain days of the week, she left mail under logs in the woods. She placed more cumbersome deliveries beside a well-known tree. At her signal, Confederate soldiers came out of hiding to retrieve the items.

Spying was a dangerous occupation at best, and these days more Federals than ever were stationed in the area. But she couldn't give up now. Her brother-in-law, Rufus Bell, was waiting for her. Together they would pass through the lines with supplies and the all-important note. Clutching her shawl around her shoulders, she smiled as she felt the piece of folded paper she had tucked in her blouse. Her cheeks warm with a mixture of fear and excitement, she hurried to meet Rufus. As they traveled through the woods, Emeline wanted to tell her brother-in-law about her precious cargo but was afraid someone would overhear. She felt unusually jittery, perhaps due to the nature of the document she carried. Suddenly, directly in their path, stood a Union soldier who was soon joined by a second, third, and fourth.

Resisting the urge to cry out, Emeline mustered a bright smile. A pretty young woman with dark hair and expressive, dark eyes, she was adept at bedazzling men, no matter whose side they were on. She was certain this bunch would let her pass.

She was wrong. They insisted she and Rufus come with them into Beaufort for questioning. Her heart in her throat, Emeline forced herself to be calm, to look innocent. What in the world was she going to do?

At the jail, the Federals searched Rufus first. Finding nothing, they released him and delegated an African-American woman to search Emeline and see if she was concealing anything. Stalling for time, Emeline protested. She would only submit to a search by a white woman, she said. Surely they would honor such a reasonable demand. To her relief, they went to find someone, leaving Emeline alone.

The note had to be completely destroyed, leaving no trace that it ever existed. Snatching the paper from its hiding place, she shoved it into her mouth and began to chew. As her teeth fought their way through the folded message, her hands tore every bit of mail she had hidden in her clothing to shreds. Let them try to piece it back together. At the sound of approaching footsteps, she chewed faster and harder and swallowed, just as a Union officer arrived with the woman who was to search her.

He saw the scraps of paper littering the floor and knew immediately what she had done. Breathless, Emeline met his angry tirade with a defiant gaze. The woman he had brought with him naturally found everything else Emeline had hidden about her person, an amazing assortment including an entire suit of clothing.

"You are under arrest," the officer announced. "You will be transported to prison at New Bern to stand trial."

Nearly faint with terror but determined to be brave, Emeline was relieved to learn that she would be allowed to spend the night at her parents' farm. After much pleading on her behalf, she got permission for her cousin, Mrs. Levi Woodburg Pigott, to accompany her to New Bern the next day.

Lodged in a bare, grim cell in New Bern, it was all Emeline could do to keep from weeping. That night, as she and her cousin lay stiffly on hard cots, Emeline wondered if she would be hanged or shot. Exhausted and unable to stay awake in spite of her fears, she drifted into an uneasy sleep. Her mind took her back to a happier time.

It was the summer of 1861, and Emeline Pigott was in love. Oh, she was fond of all the men in gray, especially those garrisoned across the creek from her family's farm near Morehead City. They had her utmost respect and sympathy. But she had recently come to the realization that Stokes McRae was different. Her relationship with him was nothing like the mild flirtations she often engaged in. At twenty-five, she was old enough to recognize real love, and this was it.

Emeline was quite accustomed to being courted. She had been invited to several social affairs by Confederate officers. But Stokes was only a private and not allowed to attend the parties and balls. Since he couldn't go, Emeline preferred to stay home. As a sign of her love, she made a Confederate flag of silk, mounted on a gold staff, for her sweetheart to carry with him.

Stokes McRae belonged to the Twenty-Sixth North Carolina Infantry, as did Emeline's cousin Gaston Broughton. Stokes had joined the Confederate army in Anson County, more than two hundred miles west of Emeline's home on the North Carolina coast. What a different world it must be that far inland, she thought, with cotton fields as far as the eye could see.

Born on December 15, 1836, in Cartaret County, North Carolina, Emeline Pigott was the daughter of Levi and Eliza Dennis Pigott. She couldn't imagine life without the sounds and smells of the mighty Atlantic Ocean. Growing up, she enjoyed frequent visits to nearby Beaufort, with its quaint, one-hundred-year-old houses. In one old cemetery there, she had been told, a man was buried upright so he could salute the king.

As a child, Emeline had listened wide-eyed to tales of ruthless pirates who raided merchant vessels along the North Carolina coast during the 1700s. They had not been content to plunder at sea but had cruised right into the harbors, huge knives clenched in their teeth. On one occasion, they had actually attacked the town of Beaufort. Terrified citizens poured into the streets, desperate to flee the assault. Even as an adult, Emeline shuddered to think of it. Now that the Southern states were at war with the North, she supposed the Yankees would do the same thing the pirates had done.

"I'm so happy I met Stokes," she told her sister Henrietta. "But I hate that it took a war to bring him this way."

In March of 1862, the call Emeline dreaded finally came. The Twenty-Sixth regiment was summoned to New Bern, thirty miles away. Union troops were approaching the town in gunboats via the Neuse River, and a strong defense would be needed. Emeline followed the men, hoping to be of help in some way. Although her soldiers in gray fought valiantly, New Bern fell to the Federals after four hours of battle. Disheartened by the loss, Emeline nevertheless breathed a sigh of relief when she learned that Stokes and Gaston had both survived. Their regiment was then sent north to Virginia.

Emeline remained in New Bern until the last train carrying the wounded had departed. She then followed the soldiers to Kinston, another thirty miles inland from her home. There she remained for several months, nursing the sick and injured.

The Twenty-Sixth fought in Virginia then returned to eastern North Carolina to protect the city of Richmond's "back door." In May of 1863, the regiment was attached to the Army of Northern Virginia. It was General Robert E. Lee's intention to take the war into enemy territory and attack them where they lived. They headed north, toward Pennsylvania.

"What a fine appearance the regiment made as it marched out from its bivouac near Fredericksburg that beautiful June morning," reported a proud member of the Twenty-Sixth. "The men beaming in their splendid uniforms; the colors flying, and the drums beating; everything seemed propitious of success."

On July 1, Stokes McRae—by then a sergeant major—and First Lieutenant Gaston Broughton took part in their regiment's assault on Federal troops posted in McPherson's Woods, near the town of Gettysburg, Pennsylvania. Again and again, the men in gray broke through the line of resistance, forcing the Unionists to pull back from their position of strength. But their success was bittersweet. Fourteen times, the regimental colors were shot down. Of the eight hundred men from the Twenty-Sixth who participated in the battle, over half were reported dead, wounded, or missing by the end of the day. Their commander, Colonel Henry King Burgwyn, Jr., had been killed leading his men to their small victory.

The Twenty-Sixth spent July 2 regrouping and resting while other units took up the challenge. Then, on the afternoon of July 3, the regiment added its numbers to the forces under Pettigrew, Pickett, and Trimble. Fifteen thousand strong, they marched for one mile across an open field toward the Union center on Cemetery Hill. Union artillery and rifle fire turned living human beings into corpses where they stood. In less than an hour, ten thousand men lay dead or wounded.

Although its colors were shot down eight times during the onrush, the Twenty-Sixth finally broke through to plant them on the Federal works. They had achieved the farthest advance of any Confederate unit during the battle. They had also suffered the highest casualties. In a letter dated July 9, 1863, General Pettigrew wrote the following to Zebulon Baird Vance, North Carolina's wartime governor and former commander of the Twenty-Sixth Regiment:

> Knowing that you would be anxious to hear from your old regiment, the Twenty-sixth, I embrace an opportunity to write you a hasty note. It covered itself with glory. It fell to the lot of the Twenty-sixth to charge one of the strongest positions possible. They drove three, and we have every reason to believe, five regiments out of the woods with a gallantry unsurpassed. Their loss has been heavy, very heavy, but the missing are on the battlefield

and in the hospital. Both on the first and third days your old command did honor to your association with them and to the State they represent.

When General Lee gathered his remaining forces and departed Gettysburg on the evening of July 4, he left behind Stokes McRae, hospitalized with a broken thigh, and Gaston Broughton, wounded in the foot and taken prisoner. The town itself, with its population of about twenty-four hundred, was left to deal with more than fifty thousand casualties, thousands of human corpses piled high, an estimated five thousand dead mules and horses, and the rest of the battle's waste and wreckage.

McRae's Company K, under Lieutenant Polk, retreated across the Potomac with only 16 of its original 103 men. In all, the rebels managed to transport several thousand of their wounded back to Virginia in a seventeen-mile-long wagon train. The captaincy of Company D was held open awaiting the return of First Lieutenant Broughton.

A fully equipped, modern hospital system would have had trouble handling the deluge of injured and dying people that filled barns, sheds, stables, schoolhouses, and homes in the vicinity of Gettysburg. In these primitive facilities, overcrowded and understaffed, confusion and chaos reigned. Unfortunately, if more than twenty-four hours elapsed between the injury and surgery, chances of survival were cut in half.

Stokes McRae, his thigh bone shattered by a Minie ball, probably underwent an amputation. Emeline Pigott would never find out if her true love died from inappropriate treatment, inadequate treatment, or lack of treatment. She knew only that his suffering ended on August 2, 1863. Her heart ached to think of him languishing in that hospital, where the babble of daily life could not be heard above the groans and shrieks of the wounded.

Word was passed that an unknown North Carolina soldier in a Gettysburg hospital had bitterly remarked "I thought I was fighting for liberty, and here I am dying like a dog." It sounded like something Stokes would say. Emeline's eyes filled with tears, but she blinked them away. She could never bring him back. But there were other things she could do.

For the time being, she remained in Kinston, where she tended sick and injured soldiers. In December, when the Federals took Kinston, Emeline made her way to Concord, more than two hundred miles west, deep into North Carolina's Piedmont Region. There she learned that Cabarrus County, where Concord was located, had once been part of Anson County, where Stokes McRae had enlisted in the Confederate army.

Concord was definitely in "the land of cotton." For Emeline, the sound of crows cawing in the fields was a poor substitute for the cries of seagulls. She missed the coast, where salty breezes blew across the wild dunes. In Concord, she met Mrs. Brett, the widow of a chaplain of the Northern army. Like Emeline, Mrs. Brett longed to return to her home. Bonded by this common desire, the two women worked their way through the Federal lines, finally arriving at the Pigott farm near Morehead City.

Emeline was happy to be back. As she gazed across Calico Creek, however, at the Union troops camping where her dear Stokes had once been stationed, she knew she must do more to help her men in gray. Soon, like numerous other Southern ladies, she was carrying mail and documents in large pockets sewn under her full skirts. According to an article that appeared in the *Greensboro Daily News* in 1963:

> She organized fishermen to meet Northern vessels in Bogue Sound and Beaufort Inlet. These fishermen would pretend to sell fish, all the while working to discover the

tonnage of each vessel, what cargo they carried, and their next destination. Emeline passed all this information to the proper civil and military authorities.

At other times, Emeline entertained Yankee soldiers at her parents' farm, distracting them long enough for her brother-in-law to carry food from the pantry to the starving Confederates hiding in the nearby woods. If she couldn't spend her days with her true love, she could at least do everything possible to help his comrades, even if she wound up in prison.

Tossing and turning that night in her jail cell in New Bern, Emeline suddenly awoke. At first she wasn't sure why. Then she instinctively covered her nose with her hand. She had smelled that noxious odor often enough, in hospitals in New Bern and Kinston. Rags soaked in chloroform were routinely used to render soldiers senseless during surgery. She had often wondered how the surgeons knew when to remove the sponge to avoid poisoning the patient.

Now, lethal chloroform fumes were filling the tiny cell where she and her cousin were imprisoned. Someone had apparently taken it upon himself to act as judge and jury, condemning Emeline to death without a hearing. Quickly she roused her companion. They broke a small hole in the window pane, then took turns breathing enough fresh air to keep from passing out. In the meantime, a guard heard the commotion and came to their aid.

Over the next month, Emeline was scheduled for trial on several occasions but never received a hearing. Meanwhile, conditions in the prison were almost unbearable. Had it not been for the thoughtfulness of New Bern's residents, she would have suffered even more. In "The Sacrifice or Daring of a Southern Woman During the War Between the States," a undated paper prepared for the Emeline Pigott Chapter of the United Daughters of the Confederacy of Morehead City, Mildred Wallace wrote:

The people of New Bern were exceedingly kind to her, especially two little Taylor boys who carried her food every day. These boys became very efficient men and one is now connected with the Sanitorium at Morganton, North Carolina. She often referred to these men in after years and was ever appreciative of their kindness to her while in prison.

During her incarceration, Emeline kept her eyes and ears open, and in doing so, learned that the note the two Northern men had given her contained false information. They had set her up. She sent out word that she wanted to see them. When they arrived, Emeline told them in no uncertain terms that if she stood trial for spying, she would cheerfully reveal their involvement. The two profiteers quickly arranged her release, and she and her cousin were sent home.

Back on the family farm, Emeline was under constant surveillance, and her house was searched regularly. Nevertheless, she managed to communicate with soldiers in faraway prison camps. One letter sent to her from Point Lookout, Maryland, on November 15, 1864, read:

Miss Emeline J. Pigott
Morehead City, N.C.

Dear Miss,

Enclosed you will find a Ring which you will please accept with my best wishes, also with the respect of Mr. Frank Hartsfield and Mr. Robert W. Humphrey—all of us are enjoying good health. You will please write us on receipt of this letter and oblige.

Very Respectfully
W. T. Weathersbee
Co. H, 5th Division
Prison Camp

A roster of North Carolina troops compiled by Louis H. Manarin lists William Thomas Weathersbee as a private in the First Regiment, Company A, the "Edgecombe Guards." As did many of the soldiers, he later served in other regiments and companies. Wounded in the left lung at Newport Barracks in 1864, he was captured and hospitalized at Morehead City where he presumably met Emeline Pigott. He was then transferred first to Fort Monroe, Virginia, and later to Point Lookout in June of 1864.

Robert W. Humphrey, another private, enlisted in Craven County, North Carolina, in 1861. He was confined at Point Lookout until February of 1865 when he gained his freedom in a prisoner exchange.

Emeline's cousin, Gaston Broughton, was confined at Fort Delaware following the Battle of Gettysburg. Regimental records show that he was transferred to Johnson's Island, Ohio, then to Baltimore, and then to Point Lookout. In June of 1865, he was released at Fort Delaware after taking the oath of allegiance to the Federal government. He wrote at least one letter to Emeline in February of 1865, and about three months prior to his release from prison, he wrote the following note:

24th Division Officers Quarters
Ft. Delaware, Ill
April 26, 1865

My Dear Cousin,
Your letter dated April 18 has just been received and

I hasten to reply I was truly glad to hear from you. As one of my Very Dear Cousins your offer to help me is a very kind one. I can say to you that it is almost impossible for me to procure a permit at present, therefore you can send me some money. You can send what amount you see proper. Money is something that I handle but little of, but if a man has money he can live pretty well by getting things from the Sutler [a civilian who provides provision at an army post]. But everything is very high. I do not know when I shall go home but after this war I intend to visit your town and then I can give my love to all my friends. Lt. J—from my company and regiment is here with me. Let me hear from you soon. Give my Rank and Regiment Company when you send the money. I am your cousin,

Gaston Broughton, Lt.
26 NC Regt, Division 24

Emeline Pigott was a member of the New Bern chapter of the United Daughters of the Confederacy and in her later years organized a chapter in Morehead City. It was named for her, and she held the title of honorary president until her death on May 26, 1919, at the age of eighty-two.

Emeline was buried in the Pigott family graveyard on the shore of Calico Creek near Morehead City. In the same cemetery lies the body of an unknown Confederate soldier, one of the first to be killed in that part of North Carolina. It was Emeline who insisted he be buried there, and she who tended his grave as long as she was physically able. The cemetery is now a historic site in Morehead City, located on what was formerly the Pigott plantation.

EMELINE JAMISON PIGOTT

In 1959, the Carteret Community Theatre dramatized Miss Emeline's courage and dedication to the Southern cause by performing a play titled *Bonnie Blue Sweetheart*, written by Ruth Pelling. ❧

SALLIE SOUTHALL COTTEN
1846–1929

Ideal Woman of the New South

*N*o two ways about it, the Exposition was going to be a sight to behold. Built on more than six hundred acres near Chicago's business district, it would contain exhibits from all over the world. At the very center, a dazzling Great White City would rise into the sky, its domes, walls, and pillars gleaming. The Midway Plaisance, an amusement park around the perimeter of the grand structures, would feature a mind-boggling assortment of activities: German beer gardens, balloon rides, a wax museum, and a Moorish palace, to name just a few. Education, entertainment, and enlightenment would be the words of the day. Scheduled to open in 1892, the fair would celebrate the four hundredth anniversary of Columbus's arrival in America—hence its name: The Columbian Exposition.

Sallie Southall Cotten could hardly wait to see the Women's Building. The Italian Renaissance-style structure would contain eighty thousand square feet of space. Located at the head of the Midway, it would house the headquarters for the Board of Lady Managers as well as special exhibits. As one of two Lady Managers from North Carolina, Sallie's role was to help oversee the presentation of women's work throughout the Exposition, as well as to organize and direct

Sallie Southall Cotten

NORTH CAROLINA COLLECTION, UNIVERSITY OF NORTH CAROLINA LIBRARY, CHAPEL HILL.

the state's exhibit. She was excited to be part of such an impressive undertaking, but a little bit uncertain about her qualifications. In a 1929 interview with Lucy Cherry Crisp for the *Charlotte Observer*, Sallie confided:

> I had never traveled much, and felt utterly unprepared to work on a board with outstanding men and women of the country. But I soon felt at home, for I discovered many who knew no more than I did. There are not so many differences in women, after all. I had kept up with things by reading and by just living, and I found that the years of home duties had fitted me for the fields of larger service.

Born Sallie Swepson Sims Southall on June 13, 1846, Sallie was the daughter of Susannah Sims and Thomas J. Southall of Lawrenceville, Virginia. The family moved across the North Carolina line to Murfreesboro when Sallie was in her teens. At age seventeen, she graduated from Greensboro Female College and became a school teacher in Edgecombe County, North Carolina.

During that time, America was deep in the trenches of the War Between the States. A little over two weeks after Sallie turned seventeen, Union forces defeated Confederate troops at Gettysburg, Pennsylvania. The war continued, finally ending in April of 1865 with General Robert E. Lee's surrender to General Ulysses S. Grant.

The following year, Sallie married Robert Randolph Cotten, a Confederate veteran from Edgecombe County. The couple lived alternately in Edgecombe County, Wilson County, and Pitt County, all on North Carolina's coastal plain. Robert first ran a mercantile business then purchased two plantations: Cottendale and Southwood.

During the first half of her marriage, Sallie's days were spent raising her children, working in her house and garden, and exercising her quick mind and strong spiritual energy on behalf of the Episcopal church where she was a member. Although nine children were born to the Cottens, only six survived past early childhood.

Sallie described this stage of her life to Lucy Cherry Crisp in 1929:

> The work of bringing up so large a family was tremendous, but I always found time to read. I kept a book in my sewing basket and read every spare minute I could find, often when I was rocking the cradle. I was writing some, too, little articles for papers and poems. . . . When I look back at those years, I see them as the most developing ones of my life. . . . Nothing has ever blessed me more than my motherhood.

As a Lady Manager for the Columbian Exposition in the 1890s, Sallie spent countless hours delving into North Carolina's rich history. In her research, she came across a fascinating tale that captured her imagination. Completely engrossed in the story, she temporarily forgot the Exposition and wandered back through time.

In her mind, she stood on Roanoke Island, off the North Carolina coast, where tropical storms had churned the sand into magnificent dunes. Ocean waves crashed against heavily-wooded shores. Gulls cawed, swooped, and plucked fish from the water with sharp beaks. The year was 1587. Sir Walter Raleigh of England had sent 117 men, women, and children to form a colony on the northern tip of the island.

It wasn't Raleigh's first attempt to tame the windswept wilderness of Roanoke. Two prior expeditions had failed to thrive there. Indeed, when the group arrived in 1587 expecting to retrieve fifteen men who had been left the year before, they found only bones, a ruined fort, and empty houses in which deer were feeding.

The newest arrivals to "Virginia," as the British called the area at the time, quickly set about restoring Fort Raleigh and the rest of the settlement built by their unfortunate predecessors. Not long after they arrived, on August 18, a baby was born to Eleanor White Dare, wife of Ananais Dare and daughter of John White, governor of the colony. The child was christened Virginia, in honor of her birthplace, which had been named for the "Virgin Queen," Queen Elizabeth of England.

Virginia Dare was the first child born to English parents in North America. On August 27, two days after her baptism, her grandfather, John White, departed for England to obtain additional supplies needed by the colonists. What happened on the island in his absence became the state's greatest unsolved mystery.

Many years after reading the story, Sallie Southall Cotten remembered it still and set about putting the tale into her own words. In 1901, in her preface to her "history-in-verse" about The Lost Colony, she wrote:

> When White reached England he found war going on with Spain. . . . Not until 1590—three years later—did he succeed in returning to America. When at last he came the colonists had disappeared, and the only clue to their fate was the word "Croatoan," which he found carved on a tree. . . .
>
> But tradition illumines many periods of the past which history leaves in darkness, and tradition tells how this colony found among friendly Indians a refuge from the dangers of Roanoak [sic] Island, and how this infant grew into fair maidenhood, and was changed by the sorcery of a rejected lover into a white doe, which roamed the lonely island and bore a charmed life, and how finally true love

triumphed over magic and restored her to human form—only to result in the death of the maiden from a silver arrow shot by a cruel chieftain.

From recent search into the subject by students of history a chain of evidence has been woven from which it has come to be believed that the lost colony . . . became a part of a tribe of friendly Croatoan Indians. . . . and that their descendants are to be found to-day among the Croatoan Indians of Robeson County, North Carolina.

Sallie presented her poem about the Legend of the White Doe in six chapters, each verse filled with vivid imagery, each line crafted gently into a hypnotic cadence. The first section, called "The Refugees," set the stage:

In the Land-of-Wind-and-Water,
Loud the sea bemoaned its sameness;
Dashing shoreward with impatience
To explore the landward mysteries.
On the sand the waves spread boldly,
Vainly striving to reacher higher;
Then abashed by vain ambition,
Glided to their ordained duty.

Sallie's treatment of the legend garnered praise from all who read it. But by that time, she had already earned a reputation as a lady of ability and accomplishment. For her contributions as a member of the Board of Lady Managers for the Columbian Exposition, she received a World's Fair medal and diploma. A press clipping she saved in her scrapbook called her "one of the most able and popular members of the board" and added "Her strongly magnetic nature makes her a central figure everywhere. Mrs. Cotten represents the ideal woman of the progressive new south in that she combines great ability with that charm of manner, that genuineness of sympathy, and that generous appreciation which marks particularly the cultivated, evolved woman of the southern section."

Due to a number of difficulties, the Columbian Exposition did not start in 1892 as planned but opened its gates in May of 1893. It was a mind-boggling experience for Sallie. In addition to taking in thousands of sights, sounds, and smells, she witnessed the first appearance anywhere of a gigantic wheel created by Pennsylvania bridge builder George W. Ferris. The Ferris Wheel sported thirty-six wooden cars. Each time a car reached the top, its occupants—up to sixty people—were treated to a view of the grounds from 264 feet in the air.

In a journal she kept during her six-month stay in Chicago, Sallie revealed conflicting feelings. While she thoroughly enjoyed the excitement and activities of the Exposition, she grew weary at times. On a number of occasions, she succumbed to illness. In the long term, however, the Exposition strongly influenced her future and the future of women across the nation.

"I could write pages as to the Exposition and its effect on me," she wrote. A journal entry from August of 1893, read:

> I saw some ladies trying a "Nickle [sic] in the Slot" machine which would give you your exact weight, play a tune, and also hand out to you a souvenir card—giving your weight and telling your fortune. I decided to try it. I slipped in my nickle—stood on the machine and duly received my souvenir. Weight 141—with this prediction on other side "For you I see a heroic effort and handsome reward."

The dizzying heights reached by the brave souls on the Ferris Wheel were nothing compared to the heights American women achieved in their quest for civil rights after the turn of the century. True to the slot machine's forecast, Sallie Southall Cotten played a significant role.

Brimming with confidence gained from her success as a Lady Manager for the Exposition, Sallie decided to open a school for young girls called the "Virginia Dare School." She saw the education of young women as one of the most important steps to be taken toward improving women's lot in life. Soon, however, she determined that another route might be equally effective.

At the Exposition, she had heard about women's clubs where women studied a variety of subjects, learned to express their ideas and goals in public, and worked together for shared causes. Even as she pondered how she might introduce this concept in North Carolina, she was asked to represent the state in Washington, D.C., where women from all over the nation were gathering to form a Congress of Mothers.

Although aristocratic in appearance, Sallie was unfailingly accessible and down-to-earth in her relationships with others. Recognized immediately as an innovator, she was elected recording secretary of the Congress of Mothers and served as an officer for fifteen years. Eventually, at the urging of Sallie and other leaders, the group developed a broader focus and changed its name to the National Congress of Mothers and Parent-Teacher Association. In 1919, Sallie gave her whole-hearted support to Mrs. David S. Yates of Charlotte in her efforts to organize a state chapter for North Carolina.

By that time, Sallie had already immersed herself in the work of the North Carolina Federation of Women's Clubs (NCFWC), which she had helped organize in 1901. She became president of the NCFWC in 1911, having earned the nickname "Mother of the

Federation." As reported by Lucy Cherry Crisp in the *Charlotte Observer* in 1929, Sallie Cotten was "determined to start a federation of women's clubs that would be uplifting and respectable." Crisp went on to write:

> Attainments of the federation under her leadership give an idea of the kind of thing she considers "respectable": The establishment of a loan fund for needy girls desiring a college education, the creation of a state library commission and the beginning of traveling libraries; influence brought to bear in the passage of a bill providing for the appointment of women on school boards.

When it came to the women's suffrage movement, Sallie was not particularly supportive at first. Her son, Bruce, elaborated on her views in his memoirs, *As We Were: a Personal Sketch of Family Life*:

> In the matter of votes for women, mother was, in the early days of the movement, against it. . . . She told me . . . upon several occasions, that she was opposed to it, because she feared it might lead to some "embarrassment of our men." "North Carolina," she said, "has made the pluckiest fight against distressing odds of any State in the South, and I don't think that we women ought to do anything that might embarrass our men politically."

At the same time, Bruce noted, his mother felt there was much lacking in the life of the average woman:

> She regretted what she regarded as the inferior role, that civilization had at this point assigned to women, and positively resented the implication of mental inferiority.

She felt that the greatest need in the world was an edu-cated, vigorous, unhampered womanhood—a woman elevated and lifted out of her hampered stagnated state into a vastly more useful field.

Sallie Southall Cotten was clever with words but also clever enough to know that words alone did not accomplish very much. She was committed to fulfilling, to the best of her ability, the de-scriptions she herself gave of enlightened womanhood. Her efforts bore great fruit when joined with other women of purpose and talent. As she wrote in her book *History of the North Carolina Federation of Women's Clubs 1901–1925*:

> What has been known as the Woman's Movement, was a revolution—bloodless but not purposeless. A new era in world history was imminent but not yet visible. . . . Everywhere woman while absorbed by the duties of moth-erhood and home-making, felt, without understanding, the inner stirrings of undeveloped powers, but was afraid of the uncharted seas. . . . The restrictive conventions of her isolated individuality gave to the women of the past what would now be called an "inferiority complex," which was simply the habit of sex-submission, from which she will ultimately be emancipated.

Eventually, Sallie did come forward in favor of giving women the vote. In fact, she described voting as a responsibility and mis-sion similar to church attendance. To her, it was also the most effec-tive way for women to help defend America against Bolshevism, which she recognized as a response to continued social injustices. Women must never permit or assist injustice, she told her audi-ences, adding "Nothing permanently good can be built on injustice.

The high aim must ever be the good of all . . . I repeat that [women] must do better than man has done or her franchise is vain."

Later, though, Sallie again found herself wondering if giving women more influence had been wise. Her son, Bruce, wrote in his memoirs: "The only time I ever discovered her faith [in her sex] wavering, was during the years immediately after the war, when the young people revolted against all conventionalities and many essential decencies."

At women's feet Sallie laid the blame for the loose morals and scandalous behavior of the "Roaring Twenties." Still, she had faith in the future, believing that mistakes often contributed to the further evolution of the human race. Sometimes, she knew, experience was the best teacher, even if it also brought pain and regret.

Up until that time, there had been many areas of life women had been prevented from experiencing. Sallie was pleased that careers other than marriage were opening up for women, yet she saw no reason to throw aside morality and motherhood.

Sallie Southall Cotten not only helped lay the foundation for the North Carolina Federation of Women's Clubs, but due largely to her dedication and ability, she helped the Federation grow steadily. In 1999, it included 211 Women's Clubs with a total membership of 7,558.

As the pandemonium of the "Roaring Twenties" began to subside, Sallie's life also calmed considerably. Sadly, she lost a son, a daughter, and her husband during the period from 1926 to 1928. In failing health, she moved to Boston to live with her daughter Sallie.

On May 4, 1929, Sallie Southall Cotten passed away. She was laid to rest beside her husband in Greenville, North Carolina. Four of her children survived her.

Even in death, Sallie continued to collect honors. Dormitories were named for her at the University of North Carolina at Greensboro and at East Carolina University in Greenville. In 1943, a Liberty Freighter named for her was launched at Wilmington after being christened by her granddaughter. The SS *Sallie S. Cotten* pulled away from shore well over two hundred miles down the coast from the tip of Roanoke Island and more than three centuries after Virginia Dare's parents first spied that island. Yet the powerful, rolling ocean waves, the salty taste of the sea breeze, and the raucous cry of the gulls would seem familiar to them even today.

In her preface to "The Legend of the White Doe," Sallie Cotten credited North Carolina's early settlers with sowing seeds for a great harvest. She noted that people of her generation were reaping that harvest centuries later. Through her own careful stewardship of that harvest—and her planting of new seeds—she left a rich legacy for the generations of North Carolinians who followed her.✤

Dr. Annie Lowrie Alexander

1864–1929

Pioneer Woman Physician

Dr. John Brevard Alexander sank into a chair in the living room of his comfortable home. His wife, Ann Wall Lowrie, could tell by the look on his face that something was troubling him. Knitting needles clicking in a light rhythm, she waited patiently for him to tell her what was on his mind.

Before long, he began to talk about his day—about a young woman who had died that afternoon. As a physician, he encountered death often enough. But this particular case, he told Ann, had been unusually difficult.

"Because I was a man, she wouldn't let me examine her, so that I could help her," he said. "If a woman doctor had been available, she might still be alive."

"What a shame!" Ann exclaimed.

"Indeed," John said. "This is 1877, Ann, not the Middle Ages, yet society still balks at the idea of a female physician. Why, even when Geneva admitted Elizabeth Blackwell thirty years ago, they did it as a joke! There was no humor in what I witnessed this afternoon."

NORTH CAROLINA DIVISION OF ARCHIVES AND HISTORY

Dr. Annie Lowrie Alexander

Upstairs, the Alexanders's thirteen-year-old daughter Annie lay awake. She often listened to her parents' conversations at night and found their quiet exchange of ideas reassuring. This time, however, her father's comments distressed her. She had heard about Elizabeth Blackwell, the Englishwoman whose name had been submitted to the students at Geneva Medical School in New York as a candidate for admission. They had thought it was a prank being played by a rival school and had voted to accept Elizabeth. Annie had to smile at that one.

She tried to picture herself in Elizabeth Blackwell's place. Even after Elizabeth graduated, she had not been allowed to practice medicine in any hospital. So she had started a clinic in New York with her sister and another woman. Then, several years ago, she had opened the Women's Medical College of the New York Infirmary.

"If it were me," Annie thought. "I would be just like her. I wouldn't give up, no matter what anyone said or did. I would get my degree so I could help people like Papa's patient."

"Ann," she heard her father say to her mother. "Do you realize what an excellent doctor our Annie would make? I could teach her the basics myself."

Annie's heard thumped. She formed the words silently: "Dr. Annie Lowrie Alexander." Was it possible? What would it be like? It was a long time before Annie fell asleep that night.

Annie Lowrie Alexander entered the world on January 10, 1864, one of six children born to John and Ann Alexander of Cornelius, North Carolina. Originally a settlement known as "Liverpool," Cornelius was about twenty miles from the city of Charlotte. "The Queen City," as Charlotte was called, had been named after Princess Charlotte Sophia, wife of England's King George III. The town was considered a "royal pain" by at least one of Great Britain's royal subjects. During the American Revolution, British commander Lord Charles Cornwallis found the residents of Charlotte somewhat less than hospitable. To his aggravation, the uncooperative Charlotteans burned their own barns in order to avoid giving his troops the supplies they demanded. In October of 1780, upon learning of the death of his colleague Major Ferguson in a battle at nearby King's Mountain, Cornwallis is said to have remarked "Let's get out of here. This place is a damned hornet's nest."

The blood of those spirited "hornets" ran in Annie Lowrie Alexander's veins. She was a member of one of Mecklenburg County's pioneer clans. Her forefathers included the Reverend Alexander Craighead and the Reverend David Caldwell, who regularly exhorted their parishioners to resist the British at every opportunity. Like her ancestors, Annie was not easily deterred once she decided what she wanted to do. In becoming a doctor, she often had to call on that revolutionary courage to keep her going.

A rigorous education by her father and a private tutor prepared Annie for enrollment in Women's Medical College in Philadelphia. Her quick mind and determined spirit saw her through the long hours of study, and she graduated in 1884 with honors. She completed a year-long internship at the college and in 1885, went before the Maryland State Board of Medical Examiners. The only woman among one hundred candidates, she earned the highest grade on the Board's test. She then became an assistant teacher of anatomy in the Women's Medical College of Baltimore, at the same time operating her own private medical practice. According to the Charlotte-Mecklenburg web-site, she practiced medicine for an entire year before earning $2.

In America in those days, scientific medicine was struggling to break through a thick fog that had settled over the country in the first half of the nineteenth century. A great many people had come to believe they could cure any illness using "common sense" treatments, without the help of licensed physicians. Patent medicines, mesmerism, phrenology, and hydropathy gained credibility. These approaches dominated until the horrifying rates of disease and death during the Civil War forced everyone to face reality. Acceptance was granted to scientists like Louis Pasteur, who disproved the theory of "spontaneous generation" of germs and Joseph Lister, who advocated antiseptic surgery. Fatal illnesses like puerperal fever, which often appeared "mysteriously" in women following childbirth, were linked with the simple fact that the doctor's hands and instruments were not clean.

As Dr. J. B. Alexander, Annie's father, wrote in his *History of Mecklenburg County*, published in 1902: "Fifty years ago but little attention was paid to the cause of the disease, but the symptoms were combatted as they should arise. Microbes did not then exist, or at least had not been discovered."

By the time Annie Lowrie Alexander began her schooling, however, training and education for physicians had advanced considerably. In 1869, Harvard's medical college extended its school year from four months to nine, began to require both written and oral examinations, and established a three-year curriculum. When Johns Hopkins University opened in 1876, its founder required clinical practice as an integral part of training.

In 1887, Annie returned to North Carolina, becoming one of the first (some say *the* first) woman to practice medicine in the South. Noted for her "femininity, gentle manners, and cultured womanhood," she hung out her shingle in Charlotte, where a hospital had been organized about ten years earlier. Established in 1876 "for the care of the aged and infirm," the Charlotte Home and Hospital initially consisted of two beds and a staff of one matron. Its first patients were called inmates, and according to Mrs. Hamilton C. Jones, one of the hospital's founders, the dear souls were brought in "under resistance so fierce that one of the two policemen which the town boasted had always to walk beside the patient." The general public viewed hospitals as places where people suffered horribly and died. At first, a guard had to be posted to discourage opponents from shooting into the building.

Fortunately, by the time Dr. Annie Lowrie Alexander arrived, the situation had improved. A new hospital building had been completed in 1878, and an addition had been built in 1882. In 1885, at long last, the city of Charlotte set aside its age-old distrust and donated $200 to the institution. Even though female physicians were still not well accepted by the general public, Annie built her medical practice slowly and surely.

Although Annie Lowrie Alexander had no partners, she relied heavily on an assistant named Conrad for many years. Unfailingly reliable and faithful, Conrad accompanied her on her rounds, making sure she reached those who needed her in a timely manner. To her, he was worth every penny she spent on his room and board. Only the choicest hay was good enough for Conrad. Conrad was Annie Alexander's horse.

So familiar was Annie's "assistant" to her community that forty years later one of Charlotte's prominent citizens, when shown a photo of "Dr. Annie" in her horse-drawn buggy, exclaimed: "Sure, I know that horse! That's Conrad. I used to feed and water him when I was a kid." Upon studying the picture more carefully, he changed his mind. "No, that's not Conrad. That horse is too high in his hindquarters. Conrad sloped off like a giraffe. That horse was before Conrad's day."

Conrad lived in a stable behind a house Annie had purchased on North Tryon Street in 1890. During that year, her parents moved into her home, so Annie could care for her mother.

Dr. Annie had her work cut out for her in Charlotte where the general environment was extremely unhealthy. A paper presented in 1906 on sanitary conditions in the Charlotte area noted that using water from contaminated supplies was causing a number of ailments, among them typhoid fever. An outbreak of malaria occurred in 1907.

Two years later, unsanitary conditions among the poorer residents of Charlotte, particularly mill workers, triggered a hookworm epidemic. In 1910, typhoid fever took hold of the city with a vengeance.

Members of the Mecklenburg Medical Society, including Dr. Annie Lowrie Alexander, continually raised the issue of public health, calling attention to the prevalence of bacteria and the lack of proper sanitation measures. In spite of their efforts, city officials seemed unresponsive. Physicians then turned to civic clubs and schools. In 1910, Dr. Annie worked with the Health Department of the Charlotte Women's Club to set up a series of public meetings on the hookworm problem.

Eventually, progress was made in health conditions and in other areas of life as well. In 1911, Annie replaced Conrad with a two-legged assistant—a teenage boy she hired to turn the crank on her new "horseless carriage." Being a modern woman, Annie had finally purchased a "locomobile," as cars were called when the first one arrived in Charlotte in 1900. Thanks to Henry Ford's ingenuity, Dr. Annie could make her rounds a bit more quickly, but the exertion required to get the automobile running irritated her lungs so severely that she had to have help.

As the saying goes, "there is nothing permanent except change," and Annie Alexander's life was no exception. In July of 1914, she read in the *Charlotte Observer* that Austria-Hungary had declared war on Serbia. The news was alarming, but it seemed unlikely that the United States would become involved in what was essentially a European conflict. Dr. Annie continued to focus her attention on her patients and the various bumps along her personal road. These included a collision between her automobile and a streetcar which resulted in bruises for Annie and serious cuts for her companion. Once she had attended to the young man's injuries, she took her medical bag firmly by the handle and walked down the block to call on the patient she had started out to visit before the accident.

In 1915, when Germany sank the *Lusitania*, a British passenger ship carrying one hundred Americans, the United States began to look more closely at what was going on in Europe. "U.S. DECLARES WAR" the headlines screamed on April 6, 1917, as America took up arms in support of Britain and France. The "European conflict" had become a World War. By November, the War Department had directed the organization of a major military base at Camp Greene near Charlotte.

Named for General Nathanael Greene, who defended Mecklenburg from British attack during the Revolutionary War, Camp Greene was home to more than sixty thousand soldiers before the war ended. They lived and worked in some one thousand tents and barracks just west of downtown Charlotte.

The year the troops began to arrive, Dr. Annie was appointed acting assistant surgeon at Camp Greene. Her duties included the medical inspection of thousands of school children at the camp. All around her, life continued to change dramatically. Electric streetcars appeared in Charlotte in 1917, prompting a mass exodus to the suburbs. The Bolsheviks took over Russia which caused further upheaval in Europe where the war raged on.

On the home front, Annie and other Charlotteans observed ten "Heatless Mondays" in response to a coal shortage early in 1918. Schools, factories, and markets were closed on "Heatless Mondays," as participants tried to turn a day of deprivation into a holiday. "Meatless days" were common as well.

To Dr. Annie's delight, in spite of wartime trials, Presbyterian Hospital was able to open a new facility in February of 1918. A grand celebration was held, featuring music by the Seventy-Seventh Field Artillery Band from Camp Greene. With a smile on her face, Annie toured the ten-patient children's ward, obstetrical ward, reading room, operating rooms, and charity wards. Word spread quickly, and by late March, patients were streaming to the new facility from all over the Carolinas. In June, twenty-six babies were born there, many of whom were children of soldiers stationed at Camp Greene.

In the fall of 1918, Annie faced a grueling test of her medical skill as a Spanish influenza epidemic began killing millions of people worldwide. Crowded army camps and cities were an ideal breeding ground for the disease. To keep the infection from spreading throughout the community, Charlotte officials closed parks, churches, schools, and other public buildings, and passed ordinances confining victims to their homes. With an average of nine men to a tent, Camp Greene was an obvious liability. The camp, which reported 204 cases of the flu, was quarantined.

Still, the disease continued its rampage. To make matters worse, pneumonia, a common complication of the flu, became a problem. Charlotte hospitals admitted people at a much faster rate than they could discharge them. Physicians worked long hours at a time, hardly noticing whether it was day or night. Many made more than one hundred calls per day. Dr. Annie pitched in, fighting exhaustion and fighting tears as she watched precious children succumb to the high fevers, vomiting, and complications of the vicious illness. Her burden was relieved somewhat during the ordeal by the assistance of Red Cross volunteers and members of other humanitarian agencies.

Influenza killed so many soldiers at Camp Greene that the undertakers were overwhelmed. Bodies were piled up awaiting boxes; coffins were stacked at the train station awaiting transportation to the soldiers' home towns. The death rate began to decline in late October, but before the disease was eradicated, more than 500,000 people died in the United States alone. The body count was almost double the number of Americans killed in World War I, which ended on November 11, 1918. Thankfully, the death toll in Charlotte was less than it would have been had improvements in public health and sanitation not been made earlier in the decade.

In addition to meeting the demands of her career as a physician, Annie devoted much of her time to a multitude of charitable causes. In the *Dictionary of North Carolina Biography*, Harold J. Dudley succinctly described her tireless commitment to her community:

> Along with her medical practice, she performed social welfare work, especially among women and girls; for many years she was on the board of managers of the Charlotte YWCA, and later she was a trustee and the examining physician for the physical education department of the YWCA. She was physician and board member of the Florence Crittendon home and a board member of the Associated Charities and of the Cooperative Nursing Association.

Annie served as president of the Mecklenburg County Medical Society several times. She was vice president of the Women Physicians of the Southern Medical Association and an honorary member of the North Carolina Medical and Southern Medical Associations. A prominent figure on the medical staff of Presbyterian and St. Peter's Hospitals, she served for twenty-three years as physician for the Presbyterian College for Women (later Queens College). The First Presbyterian Church, the Daughters of the American Revolution, the United Daughters of the Confederacy, and the Charlotte Women's Club also benefited from Annie Alexander's active involvement.

Dr. Annie died on October 15, 1929, four days after being diagnosed with pneumonia. On October 16, the *Charlotte Observer* reported:

> A factor of popular and beloved identity with the social and professional life of Charlotte is removed in the death

of Dr. Annie Alexander, after an illness so brief as to have been known by only a small portion of the population, a circumstance which accentuated the grief of the people over her passing. . . . In Charlotte, she honored her profession and in turn was honored by it. It was truly a lovable character that Charlotte is mourning today.

In January of 1940, Annie's house on Tryon Street was razed to make way for a million-dollar hotel. Before the demolition actually began, workmen tearing down the mantle happened to find an old negative glass behind it.

"The negative was developed," LeGette Blythe wrote in the *Charlotte Observer*. "It had been perfectly preserved. The picture was as good as if it had been taken yesterday. It shows 'Doctor Annie,' as everybody knew her, in her phaeton ready to make a call."

Blythe ended his article with the following comment: "And with the demolition of her old home, another Charlotte landmark passes and with its destruction the city and county move farther from contact with one of the interesting and important characters of an earlier day."

In a sense he was correct. Yet the spirit of true pioneers never dies; it is merely reborn in successive generations. Each time a woman receives a medical degree, and each time she treats a patient, Dr. Annie lives again.✤

ADELA F. RUFFIN
1871–1953

Activist, Advocate, Advisor

Adela Ruffin stepped back to get a better look at the fresh-cut spruce tree now that the decorations were in place. It was not as large and impressive as the municipal Christmas tree in Asheville's city square, from which hundreds of gifts would be distributed to the less fortunate children of the town. Nevertheless, Adela knew the gifts on her tree, though few in number, would have great meaning to those who received them.

Outside, the air was frigid. Light snow had fallen that morning, and the temperature was expected to dip into the teens that night. In marked contrast, the atmosphere inside the Phyllis Wheatley Branch of the YWCA (Young Women's Christian Association) was warm and welcoming. The old brick house at the corner of Hollywood and College had seen better days, but its interior was clean and homelike. Holiday refreshments were arranged attractively on a table. The lights on the tree twinkled brightly. The aroma of cinnamon, nutmeg, and pine flavored the air.

Gazing around the room, Adela was pleased. When she had first arrived in Asheville, about three years ago, the Phyllis Wheatley Branch had been a single room over a pharmacy on Market Street.

The current building consisted of eight rooms on two floors, and an addition was under construction.

Adela could hardly believe it was already Christmas Eve, 1925. Time had passed quickly. Although things never moved fast enough for her, she had to admit the Phyllis Wheatley Branch had come a long way. In fact, to the best of her knowledge, no other city in the South even had a YWCA for Negro women. The Phyllis Wheatley was only an auxiliary of Asheville's Central YWCA, but it was a step in the right direction. And now that the branch had more space, lodging could be offered. Adela often shared her living quarters on the second floor with Negro women from out of town, since they were not allowed to stay at local hotels.

Over the past three years, the Phyllis Wheatley had become a hub of community activity. Membership had risen steadily, and programs had been presented on important topics. In March, 125 members had performed a selection of Negro spirituals at the city auditorium to raise money for the Community Chest, a forerunner of the United Way.

Adela knew she might be considered aggressive or pushy by some, but she was determined to instill hope and pride within her people. To her, any advancement was long overdue. As she surveyed the cheery holiday setting, her heart was full of compassion for the young African-American women who would soon arrive.

There was a knock at the door. In seconds, the room was filled with the excited voices of her guests. Shivering from the frosty weather, they hugged their thin coats around them at first, then shrugged them off as the warmth of the room penetrated the chill in their bones.

Although Adela had recently turned fifty-four, she could still identify with these girls' fears and dreams. At the same time, she was keenly aware that her life had been quite different from theirs. Growing up in Norfolk, Virginia, she had celebrated holidays with her parents in the house where her family lived. These young women were homeless.

Throughout the evening, Adela listened to their girlish chatter, joined in the singing of carols, and watched with satisfaction as the young women eagerly opened the gifts placed under the tree. For this one night, they could forget the harsher aspects of their lives and be children once again. Adela's report to the Central YWCA for December 1925 read:

> A Christmas tree on Christmas eve brought seven young women to our building. Each had a gift on the tree. There were Christmas carols and refreshments. One young woman told a friend, "I cried at my work on Christmas day when I remembered how happy we were at the 'Y' the night before." Each girl was homeless—and happy because our tree was home-like.

The Phyllis Wheatley Branch of the Asheville YWCA was started in 1913 when a group of African-American women began getting together on Sunday afternoons. They decided to name their group after Phillis Wheatley, a woman who was brought to Boston in the 1700s as a slave and who eventually became known as "the first African-American, the first slave, and the third woman in the United States to publish a book of poems."

In 1922, Asheville's Central YWCA agreed to support further development of the Phyllis Wheatley Branch. An executive director was recruited from the national YWCA headquarters in New York. Her name was Adela F. Ruffin.

Born in Norfolk on November 18, 1871, Adela was the daughter of Ottaway Francis Ruffin, Jr., a barber and post office clerk, and Annie Elizabeth Langley Ruffin, who ran a grocery store. According to family records compiled by Adela's nephew, C. Bernard

Ruffin, Ottaway, his mother, brother, and sister had been slaves of Ann Camp, a lawyer's widow, who freed them in 1848 when she died, leaving "a small sum trust to maintain the women." Adela's grandfather, Ottaway Ruffin, Sr., descended from the Powhatan Indians. His wife, Elizabeth Cheeseman Ruffin, worked as a nurse, ran a station on the Underground Railroad, and helped found the Bank Street Baptist Church in Norfolk. Adela had two brothers: Herman, who died at a young age, and Caulbert Bernard.

According to family tradition, Adela was in the first graduating class of Norfolk Mission College, a school founded by the Presbytery of Pittsburgh in 1883. In 1899, she was hired as a teacher and "Lady Principal" at what is now Winston-Salem State University in North Carolina. Designed at first to teach African-American boys and girls the manual arts and home economics, the school was chartered in 1897 as Slater Industrial and State Normal School. That institution's records state that Adela was paid $135 per year. The school's motto "Enter to Learn . . . Depart to Serve" was in keeping with Adela's own philosophy.

It is not known exactly when Adela Ruffin moved to New York, but she was living there in 1922 when she was contacted on behalf of the Phyllis Wheatley Branch of the Asheville YWCA. During the Roaring Twenties, New York was considered by many to be "the cat's meow," "the berries," "the bee's knees," or any one of a multitude of other superlatives. More than likely, Adela had mixed views about that. On the positive side, Harlem was fast becoming a mecca for African-American literature and music. At the same time, however, morals in nearly every segment of society seemed to be plunging toward a record low.

Adela believed firmly in rules, regulations, and proper manners. In the words of Dolores Carnegie, a teenager in Asheville during Adela's administration: "My friends and I knew exactly what

Miss Ruffin expected. We used to say 'She won't put up with no messy mess.'"

When Adela arrived in Asheville, she found a city bustling with activity, eager to leap headlong into the future. Although certainly not as cosmopolitan as New York, Asheville had a spark about it that promised great things. The juxtaposition of past, present, and future was illustrated clearly in one photograph taken during that "roaring" decade. It showed an ox cart drawn up to a railway crossing with a gas station for the new "horseless carriages" in the background.

One of Asheville's best features was its strong medical community which had begun developing early in its history. In 1885, a group of women known as the Ladies of the Flower Mission had opened a charity hospital. In 1900, the Sisters of Mercy, a Catholic religious order, opened a tuberculosis (TB) sanatorium. During the first two decades of the 1900s, Asheville nurtured hundreds of people who sought the fresh mountain air as a treatment for TB, also called "consumption" and "the great white plague."

Sanatoriums helped people heal by isolating the sick from the general population and by providing enforced rest and a proper diet. This approach controlled the disease somewhat until a cure could be discovered. By the time Adela Ruffin held her Christmas Eve party in 1925, existing treatments were working well enough that the *Asheville Citizen* was able to report "Tuberculosis is no slight infection but neither is it a horrible fatality."

Oddly enough, health concerns also played a role in the birth of Asheville's magnificent Grove Park Inn: "the finest resort hotel in the world." Built of massive granite boulders, the inn opened its doors in 1913. Its creator, Edwin Wiley Grove of Tennessee, moved to Asheville because of his wife's health. The Grove Park Inn was part of a tourist industry in Asheville that grew by leaps and bounds between 1850 and 1920. Many of the town's African-Americans arrived during that time to take advantage of job opportunities. As was the case in cities all across the country, they lacked a number of the advantages white citizens took for granted. Lucy Mae Harrison, an Asheville native born in 1907, summarized the situation: "It was a time in which the black Community was ruthlessly deprived. No Negro school in the region had a gymnasium nor an auditorium. All avenues of advancement seemed to be closed. Despair and resignation clutched the hopes and aspirations of the Community."

Enter Adela Ruffin. A large, fairly heavy woman in her early fifties, Adela had a light-tan complexion and deep voice. She was a dignified and imposing figure, and as Asheville resident Gladys Kennedy observed, "Her personality was larger than she was." Once in town, Adela saw a million things that needed to be done. The minutes of Asheville's Central YWCA for December of 1923 stated:

> Mrs. Wallace Davis, Chairman of Phyllis Wheatley Committee, reports phenomenal development of the work during the year. There has been an exact doubling of the membership and a most gratifying increase of interest in the work by all members of the colored race. This has been due largely to the unusually efficient work of the capable Miss Adela Ruffin, whom the Asheville Branch was fortunate enough to secure from the national headquarters in New York.

"Miss Ruffin . . . has the keen insight, the alertness, the information and dedication of an ideal leader," read the minutes from October 13, 1926.

Even a partial list of Adela's activities in the 1920s and 1930s will serve to illustrate the extent of her energy and commitment.

She organized a health council, asking each of the town's religious leaders to observe a "health Sunday." School children were offered prizes for essays on "The Prevention and Cure of TB." She not only attended but was one of the speakers at the Church Women's Inter-racial State Conference in Durham in 1928. Her topic: "What the Colored Girl Wants from Her Employer."

Understanding that employment was a two-way street, Adela acted as an "agent" for young people who sought jobs as chauffeurs, maids, cooks, laundresses, and gardeners for Asheville's wealthier residents. The employers knew Adela's standards were high and trusted her judgment. She also served as chair of the African-American division of the Community Chest.

Under Adela's guidance, each school formed a YWCA Girl Reserve Club. The impact of this group was such that seventy years later, at the age of eighty-six, Lucy Harrison still remembered the Reserve Code of Behavior taught her by Adela Ruffin:

Gracious in Manner
Impartial in Judgement
Ready for Service
Loyal to Friends
Reaching Toward the Best
Earnest in Purpose
Seeking the Beautiful
Eager for Knowledge
Ready for Service
Victorious over Self
Ever Dependable
Sincere at All Times.

The Phyllis Wheatley Branch also sponsored camping trips

which provided an opportunity to socialize and learn inter-dependence. Everyone had duties to perform, including Adela, who was chief cook.

A large recreation room erected on the College Street site was used for club meetings, parties, teas, and other co-ed social and educational functions. Within its walls met groups with intriguing names like "The Modern Priscillas," "The Idle Hour," "The Plea-sure Seekers," "The Cosmopolite Club," "The Plant, Flower and Fruit Guild," and the "Negro Women's Federated Club." Tennis, basketball, and dancing took place in the gymnasium.

Sunday vesper services at the branch drew a crowd, as did semi-monthly current events forums. In November of 1932, 1,126 people attended activities at the branch. The Phyllis Wheatley became *the* place where African-Americans gathered for enlightenment as well as entertainment.

In Lucy Harrison's words: "It was a microcosm of Negro Asheville." Of Adela Ruffin, Lucy said,

> She was the strongest black woman in town. She suc-ceeded in portraying the needs of the black Community to the power structure. Her vision revolutionized black life in Asheville." Due largely to Adela's efforts, Lucy added, "The hopelessness and resignation that threat-ened to stifle the vitality and creativity of the Commu-nity subsided.

"Miss Ruffin was quite a distinguished person to me," said Dolores Carnegie, a teenager in 1920s Asheville. An only child, Dolores appreciated the chance to interact with other young people through Adela's programs at the Phyllis Wheatley. Adela was "like a mother hen, directing everything," Dolores added. "She was also very articulate, a good speaker."

In light of Adela's accomplishments and the many positive comments made about her, she more than likely expected to continue her role with the Phyllis Wheatley until she reached an advanced age. Instead, she was prevented from doing so by an unfortunate turn of events. The Committee of Management for the Phyllis Wheatley included the following note in its records for November of 1935:

> Since there can only be one Y.W.C.A. in a community and one Board of Trustees for the Y.W.C.A., it is recommended that two colored women and one colored man, serving for the Phyllis Wheatly [sic] Branch, act as co-trustees on the Board of Trustees of the Central Association. It is recommended that the By-Laws of the Phyllis Wheatly Branch be revised to conform to the By-Laws of the Central Association.

In January of 1936, the minutes stated that "It is now understood that the local Branch [The Phyllis Wheatley] is not correctly a Y.W.C.A. branch and never has been, as certain rulings stipulated by the National Board had never been carried out or met."

In February, a motion carried "that the Phyllis Wheatly [sic] Branch be notified that they are no longer a Branch of the Asheville Young Women's Christian Association; as the Branch has not, and will not, conform to the policies and regulations of the Central Association."

The minutes of May 20, 1936, reported approval of a recommendation "that all relations with the Branch be severed entirely."

Almost a year later, in April of 1937, the Central YWCA discussed reorganizing the Phyllis Wheatley Branch. It was decided to "wait for the present secretary to resign before plans for reorganization are perfected."

In May 1938, Adela was asked to relinquish her position with the Phyllis Wheatley. Central Association minutes referred only to an apparent lack of willingness to "work out the problem." By August, she was no longer with the branch.

Many of her friends felt she had been treated unfairly. One commented, "She was forceful, and they began to cut her down." Another said someone in an important position with the Central Association disliked Adela. Racism may have played a part. If so, it was merely a sign of the times. Certainly, Adela Ruffin had encountered that particular enemy more than once. Lucy Harrison described one upsetting incident:

[Miss Ruffin] escorted an invited group of Phyllis Wheatley teenagers to the Lake Junaluska Religious Assembly to sing. Transportation was limited. Neither she nor the girls owned a car. The bus companies were privately owned and operated. Negro passengers were not accepted, hence, only train transportation was available. The schedule consisted of an early morning departure and a late afternoon return. On the day of the sing, the girls arose early and walked to the Phyllis Wheatley. Miss Ruffin hired a taxi to take the girls to the station. The short distance from Asheville to Junaluska made arrival early. No eating facilities were available to Negroes. No thought of the well-being or hunger of the group arose in the minds of the assembly members. Shortly after midday the girls sang; the audience applauded and with smiles dismissed the group. By late afternoon the girls were famished, hungry, and angry. Finally, the train arrived. On the return to Asheville Miss Ruffin escorted the girls to a negro cafe and bought them food before returning them home. Similar racist incidents occurred throughout the years of her administration.

One cannot help but imagine the glowing remarks the assembly members made over their substantial evening meal about the "charming Negro singing group." The Emancipation Proclamation had set African-Americans free in 1863. Over half a century later, that freedom still didn't include equality or even the right to common courtesy.

Whatever the reasons for Adela's dismissal in 1938, her role with the Phyllis Wheatley was at an end. In spite of what had to be an extremely disappointing development for her, she remained in her adopted town. For a time, she worked for Dolores Carnegie's uncle as a companion to his wife, who was in poor health.

Adela was also an active member of the Calvary Presbyterian Church and played the organ during services. Helen Bronson, who was a small child in the 1940s, remembers Adela Ruffin as a senior citizen, wearing a calico or flowered dress, her voice loud and strong as she sang her favorite hymns.

Adela herself suffered from poor health during her last years, Lucy Harrison recalled. When she died in November of 1953, she was quite frail. She was buried in Asheville, the town she had served so well.

For a total of approximately fifty years, the YWCA in Asheville, like many organizations, was a "house divided." It consisted of a "black" and "white" version of everything: two buildings, two boards, two membership lists, two budgets, two sets of committees, two sets of classes, two summer day camps, two annual meetings. A year after Adela Ruffin died, an African-American woman was elected to the Board of Directors of the Central Association, a joint Public Affairs Committee was formed, and an African-American Executive

Director was hired. Work had begun in earnest toward a unified association. Today, of course, the Asheville YWCA serves all races and nationalities, fulfilling its mission as one body.

Like most people, Adela had her shortcomings. Even so, she was long on compassion and ambition. Eloquent, sensitive, and charismatic, she was the driving force behind everything the Phyllis Wheatley became and everything it represented to the African-American community.

"Nobody other than my immediate family has meant more to me than Miss Ruffin," said Lucy Harrison.

According to Lucy, one of the young men Adela encouraged to take a leadership role in his youth was Albert E. Manley, who served on the Community Chest team following his graduation from college. Manley went on to become a high school principal, university professor, and, finally, president of Spelman College in Atlanta, one of the nation's most prestigious African-American schools.

Lucy herself has made good use of the values she learned from Adela Ruffin. After graduating from college, she taught high school English and later served as assistant professor of English at Morgan State University in Baltimore, Maryland. One of Lucy's students, Harlow Fullwood, Jr., became an extremely successful entrepreneur. He and his wife created the Fullwood Foundation, which raises funds for scholarships and awards grants to organizations that provide human services.

"Such was the impact of Miss Ruffin's vision, character, leadership, and personality," Lucy said.

The old brick house on Hollywood and College is long gone, demolished to make way for progress. The Phyllis Wheatley Branch of the Asheville YWCA exists no longer, but Adela Ruffin's work lives on.✤

ANNIE WEALTHY HOLLAND
1873–1934

Woman of Peaceful Power

In the dark fens of Dismal Swamp
The hunted Negro lay:
He saw the fire of the midnight camp
And heard at times a horses tramp,
And bloodhounds distant bay.

Annie Wealthy Holland shivered even though she was sitting in a warm, cozy room. The words of "The Slave in the Dismal Swamp" gave her a chill. Written in 1842 by Henry Wadsworth Longfellow, the poem painted such a vivid, disturbing picture, Annie couldn't help wondering how many fugitive slaves had made their way into the swamp never to be seen again.

All her life, Annie had lived near the Dismal Swamp. Covering land in several North Carolina and Virginia counties, it was a world of intriguing beauty and poisonous splendor, inhabited by snakes, insects, birds, bears—and secrets. Over the years, quicksand and heavy underbrush had devoured many an interloper. The acidic water, stained dark by juniper and cypress roots, was said to be

NORTH CAROLINA DIVISION OF ARCHIVES AND HISTORY

Annie Wealthy Holland

magical. Annie pushed her glasses up higher on her nose and continued reading:

> A poor old slave, infirm and lame;
> Great scars deformed his face;
> On his forehead he bore the brand of shame,
> And the rage that hid his mangled frame
> Were the livery of disgrace.

The reference to an old slave made Annie think of her grandfather, Friday Daughtry. She was thankful that his master had been
kind to him and to his parents before him. Instead of dying in a
Godforsaken place like the Dismal Swamp, Friday had been set free
in 1867, after the War Between the States. His former owner, Mr.
Wealthy, had given him a mule, a cow, and twenty acres of land in
Isle of Wight County, Virginia.

In 1869, Friday's eldest son, John, had married Margaret Hill.
A few years later, their first child was born. They named her "Annie
Wealthy," out of respect for the mistress of the Wealthy plantation.
Friday Daughtry lived a good many years after the war, although he
did not survive to see the new century. His death had brought Annie
great sorrow, but she was relieved that it had been more peaceful
than that of the slave in Longfellow's poem. Tears filled her eyes as
she read the last verse:

> On him alone was the doom of pain,
> From the morning of his birth;
> On him alone the curse of Cain
> Fell like a flail on the garnered grain,
> And struck him to the earth.

Annie closed her book. It was true that the Dismal Swamp had served as a place of refuge for runaways, often doubling as their graveyard, but those days were gone. The twentieth century was entering its twelfth year, and Annie preferred to look to the future.

She set the book aside and stretched. Winter's early evening shadows had fallen across the room long ago, and it was time to prepare for bed. A good night's rest was important to Annie, not only because she had to get up early in the morning, but because she still felt the lingering effects of a case of malaria she had suffered in her teens. Her current job as a supervisor for more than twenty-two schools across the border in Gates County, North Carolina, required physical and mental energy. She couldn't afford to shortchange herself on sleep.

The oldest of seven children, Annie had always known the meaning of hard work. When her parents divorced, her mother remarried and moved the family to Southampton County, Virginia. There, Annie struggled to balance her studies with her responsibilities at home, which included taking care of her younger brothers and sisters.

Before too long, Annie's grandfather, sensing her frustration at her heavy load, brought her back to his farm to live and attend school. She learned how to grow sweet potatoes and peanuts and gained valuable understanding of the life led by poor rural farmers. She also observed that more and more Negroes were graduating from high schools, normal institutes, and colleges. With their new qualifications, they were taking the place of white teachers in Negro schools. This excited and inspired Annie.

Following the war, Friday Daughtry had made good use of the property given to him by his former master and had acquired an additional 130 acres of land. He fared well enough to send sixteen-year-old Annie to Hampton Normal and Agricultural Institute.

Hampton had been established in 1868 by General Samuel Chapman Armstrong who wanted to offer ex-slaves the kind of education that would help them become productive members of society. Located in Hampton, Virginia, the Institute boasted Booker T. Washington, founder of Tuskegee Institute, as one of its graduates.

After completing her public school requirements, Annie entered Hampton. It was everything she had hoped it would be. She could easily identify with Booker T. Washington's comments about the school: "Amid Christian influences I was surrounded by an atmosphere of business, and a spirit of self-help that seemed to awaken every faculty in me and cause me for the first time to realize what it means to be a man instead of a piece of property."

Unfortunately, near the end of Annie's first year at Hampton, her grandfather's health failed, and he was unable to support her education further. To make matters more difficult, Annie herself was not well. That summer, at the suggestion of some of her teachers, she took a "light occupation" in New York, caring for a three-year-old girl.

By carefully saving what she earned, Annie was able to pay for another year at Hampton. Once again, she thrived in the atmosphere of learning and discipline. Upon successfully completing her second term, she returned to work for the same New York family. During her stay, their eight-year-old daughter was injured in a fall and would allow no one but Annie to nurse her. It took all of Annie's strength to care for the child. By the time the little girl was well, Annie's own health was failing. She required several months of medical care. To her great disappointment, she had to face the fact that she would not be able to attend Hampton that fall.

Following a battle with malaria, the residual effects of which plagued her most of her life, Annie was asked to take charge of a school in her home county. She passed the required examination and received a certificate to teach second grade. The term went very well with Annie at the helm, and she began to imagine herself going back to Hampton.

But circumstances wreaked havoc with her hopes. Her mother died very suddenly shortly after school closed for the summer. Annie's three youngest brothers and sisters, including a one-year-old child, were left without anyone to care for them.

In October of 1914, in a long letter to Dr. H. B. Frissell, principal of Hampton Institute, Annie explained how she fared following her mother's death: "I then gave up all hope of ever returning to Hampton, for I knew I had to be mother for these children. My grandparents were old and feeble, especially my grandmother. My stepfather was a drunkard and did not support his family at all."

The letter went on to mention her marriage in 1888 to Hampton Institute graduate Willis B. Holland as well as courses she had taken at other schools. She had received a diploma from Virginia Normal Industrial Institute and earned a first grade certificate. After teaching for a number of years, she had assisted her husband who was a school principal. In 1898, she had taken a position teaching "in the country," about ten miles from her home in Franklin, Virginia.

Annie knew her new students would be poor, and she was not surprised when they showed up for class that fall barefoot and in worn-out pants and dresses. At least they came to school regularly, and that was what mattered to Annie. However, one day, about two months into the term, Annie arrived to find her schoolroom nearly empty. Was everyone sick, she wondered? What could the problem be?

As she removed the coat she had worn to protect herself against winter's first chill, she suddenly understood. Most of her students went barefoot because they had no shoes. The clothes they wore in warm weather were the only garments they owned. On extremely cold days, they were simply unable to attend school.

Annie knew these children could not make much progress in their education if they missed class every time the temperature plunged. In her experience, poverty was often due to laziness, but after visiting her students' homes, she realized people in this community had no way to better themselves. She wanted to help them.

In the meantime, Annie obtained a donation from a woman outside the area and bought shoes for several children. With other contributions, she purchased flannel to make a few warm dresses. Knowing that individual African-Americans could not afford the large tracts of land being sold by property owners, she persuaded them to purchase land as a group.

In 1905, Annie returned home. Her husband had resigned as principal of his school, and Annie applied for the position. She was accepted, and by her fifth year, enrollment had increased from 118 to 148. "Ours is the largest colored school in the county," she wrote in 1909.

October of 1911 heralded a new phase of Annie Wealthy Holland's life. She became a teaching supervisor in North Carolina with the task of ensuring that African-American students in Gates County received a well-rounded education. Trekking from school to school, she provided instruction in practical areas like cooking and sewing, critically-needed supplements to academic subjects. As she had in Virginia, she encouraged Gates County communities to pool their resources and energy to improve health conditions and raise their standard of living.

Annie's role as a supervisor was supported by the Jeanes Fund, a $1 million private trust founded in 1907 to promote rural Negro education. Anna T. Jeanes, a Quaker from Philadelphia, started the fund to help small schools struggling to survive without assistance from philanthropic organizations or the state. Working with Booker T. Washington, she established a Board of Trustees to direct the use of her money. The Jeanes supervisors were to serve as consultants and assistants to teachers, many of whom had little training. Washington himself sat on the Jeanes Fund Board and before long, supervisors had been placed all over the South. By 1914, Annie Wealthy Holland was one of 118 Jeanes teachers covering 119 southern counties.

An article posted on the University of South Carolina website stated:

> The Jeanes Supervisors had their work cut out for them. They often had to teach in one-room schoolhouses or schools held in churches. The school year lasted only about seven months, one former Supervisor remembers, because children had to help harvest the crops in the fall. Black schools had few books and those they did have were usually second-hand. Jeanes teachers did more than just teach, or supervise vocational education programs. They were heavily involved in the communities in which they lived and worked.

As a Jeanes supervisor, Annie was instrumental in raising money, encouraging parents, and setting up meetings for teachers at the schools under her supervision. So competent was she in this role that, in 1915, she was asked to serve as the State Home Demonstration Agent for North Carolina. Originally funded by the North Carolina Colored Teachers Association and the Jeanes Fund, the position was later incorporated into the state educational organization. Annie herself held the post for thirteen years.

In her role as State Home Demonstration Agent, Annie was required to visit and provide assistance to nineteen county training schools, ten city schools, and three state normal schools. A typical schedule called for her to visit twenty-one counties in thirty-five days. She organized reading circles and teacher training groups and gave inspirational speeches in churches. Eventually, forty-five county supervisors reported to her. Yet no matter how successful she became, she always regretted not graduating from Hampton. At the end of her letter to Dr. Frissell in 1914, she wrote:

> I've so often felt that I'd give anything to have a diploma from Hampton. I prayed a great deal about it even when I was a girl. I could never understand why I had such obstacles. Dr. Frissell, I'm sure I've taken too much of your valuable time in relating a story so insignificant, but doing so I feel will help me to do what I've tried to all these years—lay it at the feet of Jesus.

Perhaps the most important of all of Annie's skills was her knack for diplomacy. With her natural poise and grace, she served effectively as a liaison between black teachers, white superintendents, parents, and the predominately white community. She seemed to have a gift for negotiating, soothing ruffled feathers, and getting adversaries to see each other's point of view.

N. C. Newbold, the director of the division of Negro education in the North Carolina State Department of Public Instruction said:

> In a high degree she was a peacemaker and organizer of real ability. Frequently superintendents would write when there was some difficulty in a school and request that we send Mrs. Holland to iron out the difficulties. She went, and in practically every case peace and harmony were restored and the work went happily on.

Annie's belief in the power of cooperation led her to promote the idea of an organization that would bring parents and teachers into closer personal contact. In the early 1920s, she met with Frances Renfrow Doak of Raleigh, chair of an advisory committee set up to assist her in organizing a Negro Parent-Teacher State Association. Mrs. Doak later noted:

> Mrs. Holland was a masterful leader, and well do I remember our first conference. She had everything planned to the smallest detail, and presided with dignity and ability. In fact, I have known few more capable women, and during the years I saw her work so purposefully and successfully for her race, my respect and admiration for her constantly deepened.

In April of 1927, representatives from all areas of the state attended a meeting in Raleigh to finalize plans for the new organization. The delegates represented 770 associations with a total membership of more than ten thousand people. One year later, the first annual meeting of the North Carolina Congress of Colored Parents and Teachers was held. By that time, membership had risen to well over fifteen thousand. As reported in N. C. Newbold's *Five North Carolina Negro Educators*, published in 1939, the group's objectives were to raise the standards of home life, bring home and school into closer relation, and develop a united effort to secure the highest level of physical, mental, moral, and spiritual education for every child.

Annie Wealthy Holland's career was not glamorous by today's standards. Her appearance was quite plain. In disposition, she was unassuming, tactful, and cheerful. A woman of subtle strength and quiet courage, she moved mountains an inch at a time. As observed in Newbold's *Five North Carolina Negro Educators*:

It is significant that this devoted servant of public education was not fully appreciated until the final chapter of her life was written and her peaceful power and unpretentious leadership manifested itself no more in the midst of a large circle of friends and associates. Beloved of Negroes and whites alike, it was not realized how great were her labors and influence until she was with them no more.

Annie Wealthy Holland collapsed and died suddenly on January 6, 1934, as she was addressing a group of teachers in Louisburg, North Carolina. Her body was taken by train to Franklin, Virginia, where she was buried next to her husband, Willis B. Holland, who had died nine years earlier.

A memorial service for Annie in Raleigh drew eight hundred people, including several state officials. Governor Ehringhaus observed: "She has left behind her a record of service to the state, the educational system, the people, that is commendable in every way."

In 1938, ten years after the founding of the North Carolina Congress of Colored Parents and Teachers, the organization's annual meeting was held at Shaw University in downtown Raleigh. During that gathering, a tree was planted on the campus in Annie's memory.

Like the Dismal Swamp, Annie Wealthy Holland belonged to both Virginia and North Carolina. Unlike the swamp, there was nothing dismal about her. With a "ready smile and kindly greeting," she brought the joy of achievement and hope for the future to everyone she touched.✤

MARY T. MARTIN SLOOP, M.D.

1873–1962

Grand Lady of the Blue Ridge

*T*he young man on the makeshift operating table was in bad shape. Dr. Mary Sloop held her breath as her husband, Dr. Eustace Sloop, made an incision. She stifled a gasp of dismay. Angry red inflammation and signs of infection told her the patient's appendix had ruptured; his condition was even more serious than she had feared.

To make matters worse, the operating suite was in an unfinished dormitory with a few boards thrown down to create a temporary "floor." They had a roof over their heads but no walls to shield them from the brisk mountain air. Flickering kerosene lamps were the only source of light. It was 1908, and although the village of Plumtree, North Carolina had many charming features, electricity was not one of them.

Around the operating table stood the patient's father and several friends. They had gathered to see how "those young doctors" would do. Their expressions were grim. Their loaded shotguns stood nearby. Yet this was where she and "Doctor," as she called her husband, had chosen to live. They loved the mountains and were determined to help these people and to learn from them.

Mary T. Martin Sloop

NORTH CAROLINA COLLECTION, UNIVERSITY OF NORTH CAROLINA LIBRARY, CHAPEL HILL

Mary's mind replayed the events of the preceding afternoon. About a dozen rugged men had tramped up to the door of the Sloops' tiny office. Mary knew she would never forget the sight of the strong, tough-muscled blacksmith writhing in pain on a stretcher.

"He's got somethin' awful wrong in his belly," said the young man's father. "And I've seen lots of them die with that. But I b'lieve you could cut him open and take it out, whatever it is. So I brung him to you. Just open him up."

It wasn't quite that easy. Being general practitioners, the Sloops were not prepared to do major surgery. But the nearest surgeon was far away, over roads that were almost nonexistent in places, so Mary set to work. First, she improvised a sterilizing device from a tin pan and an empty lard can. Then, she and Doctor spent most of the night sterilizing instruments one or two at a time on a two-burner oil stove. At daybreak, they donned gowns and masks they had brought with them from medical school.

Meanwhile, a crowd had gathered. Mary soon realized that not everyone was offering support and encouragement. In fact, several men told the patient's father he was foolish to let these young doctors "practice" on his son.

"They'll kill him," said one. "He won't never wake up."

Secretly, Mary wondered if she and Doctor were up to the task, but she didn't let on. Later, she recounted the experience in the book *Miracle in the Hills*, written with LeGette Blythe:

The operation went slowly but steadily. It seemed a mighty long time to me. We had found a terrible situation in that abdomen and privately wondered if the young man would live overnight. But we didn't forget what we had been taught to do, nor did we forget how we had been taught to pray. So we went ahead with prayers in our hearts, because we knew it was a crucial time. . . . It frightened me a bit to see them come with shotguns and rifles; but I hadn't been in the mountains long before I learned that the men generally traveled with guns on their shoulders so as to be able to get a shot at a squirrel or a wildcat or anything else that might come along. . . . The operation was a success. The young man survived the night and quickly began to mend. Within a few weeks he was ready to go back to blacksmithing.

It was just one of countless occasions when the Sloops relied on a combination of prayer and skill. On each occasion, they grew in both knowledge and spirit.

Learning came naturally to Mary Martin Sloop. Born on March 9, 1873, she grew up in North Carolina's Piedmont region, between the mountains and the coastal plain. Her father taught geology and chemistry at Davidson College, a small Presbyterian institution. One of ten children, Mary was mentally and spiritually precocious. At the age of five, impressed by visiting missionaries, she decided that someday she would be a medical missionary to Siam.

When she was seven years old, Mary conducted Sunday School classes for the children of the family's cook. Seventy years later, she still loved to relate how Ptolemy Philadelphus White, one of her early "pupils," became the first registered pharmacist of the colored race in South Carolina.

Time passed, and Mary discovered that her denomination—Southern Presbyterian—had no missionaries in Siam. Undaunted, she decided to go to Africa instead. She was still determined to study medicine, even though she knew her mother, a most genteel Southern lady, would be appalled.

After graduating from Statesville Female College for Women in 1891, Mary focused her attention on caring for her mother who had become seriously ill. At the same time, she took a few classes at

Davidson College, primarily pre-med, although she did not share that fact with her mother. Mrs. Martin insisted that her daughter study French, a more ladylike subject.

Her mother's illness lasted twelve years. In 1903, when Mrs. Martin passed away, Mary prepared to actively pursue her dream. To her great disappointment, she learned that she would not be allowed to study anatomy at Davidson College. "It wasn't considered proper at all for me to go into a dissecting room with all those naked cadavers lying about on the dissecting tables! That indeed would have been highly unladylike. The neighbors would never have recovered from the shock of hearing about it. . . ."

Mary enrolled in the Women's Medical College of Pennsylvania, where the cadavers were presumably less offensive. Following graduation in 1906, she completed a one-year internship at the New England Hospital for Women and Children in Boston. She then took a position as the first resident physician at Agnes Scott College in Georgia. Her dream of becoming a missionary to Africa was doused at the age of twenty-nine when she was told she was too old to learn a foreign language and would surely be unable to stand the rigors of a tropical country.

During her time in Pennsylvania, Mary had kept in touch with Eustace Sloop, a young man who had first caught her attention in 1893 as a Davidson freshman. She and "Sloop," as she called him at the time, had become reacquainted in 1902 when he returned to Davidson College to study medicine. Through correspondence and visits in Philadelphia, their relationship blossomed. They shared a desire to be medical missionaries, to use their education and skill to help people. After "Sloop" earned his medical degree, Mary gave him a different nickname—"Doctor"—in recognition of his new and more dignified station in life.

Early in the morning on July 2, 1908, Mary and "Doctor" became husband and wife. The wedding took place in a little church in Blowing Rock, North Carolina, where Mary's family had a summer home. Local children decorated the chapel with mountain flowers and evergreens, and a family friend performed the ceremony. The bride and groom departed on horseback for a honeymoon trip that ended in Plumtree, North Carolina. There they began their eventful life together. In 1909, their daughter Emma was born, followed three years later by a baby boy they named Will.

Emma remembers riding horseback behind her father. "I was about two and a-half, I guess. It was raining, and I was peeking out from under a poncho. We were moving from Plumtree to Crossnore. I could see the oxen following behind us, pulling our furniture on a sled."

No less remarkable than her mother, Emma was about seven when she first learned how to administer anesthesia to surgery patients. She became quite skilled at letting just the right amount of ether drip onto the cloth covering the patient's face. Emma often went with her father on his rounds.

During the more than fifty years following her marriage, Dr. Mary Martin Sloop raised her daughter and son, served as an able partner in her husband's medical practice, and fought for better educational opportunities for the children of the valley. She directed the construction of greatly needed buildings for school and worship and waged a war against moonshine. As she reported in *Miracle in the Hills*:

> Many young boys would help their daddies or uncles at the stills at night. Now and then they'd get in fights, and sometimes there were killings. We didn't have feud murders in our area, but we had liquor murders. . . . Occasionally it might be a boy in his teens who was killed, a boy who should have been in school and not out at a still.

The mountain people had pitifully small incomes, and a large part of the little money they received came from making liquor. Mary was convinced there must be an alternative, but she began to see part of the problem when a man in the community complained that he had planted too many potatoes.

"I'm going to have nigh on to forty bushel left over," he said.

"Why, Mr. Jim," she told him, "that's an advantage. You can sell those potatoes! They buy a lot of 'em down in my country."

"But I can't git to it," Jim said. "I'd tear my wagon to pieces to go over them roads."

He had a point. In addition, by the time the potatoes made the day-long trip in a wagon over the rough roads, they were chilled and much less attractive to the buyers who wanted to use them as seed potatoes.

In this situation, Mary saw yet another challenge that simply must be met. Year in and year out, she attended meetings that were likely to influence the building of roads in Avery County. She often rode her horse to the nearest railroad station, left the horse there, and took the train the rest of the way to the meeting.

Once again, her persistence and dedication bore fruit. In her own words, "it took work, it took vigilance, it took constant pushing." But before too long, a new road wound its way up into the mountains. Trucks soon rumbled over it, hauling potatoes, cabbages, and beans to market, where they brought a fine price.

To Mary, the hills of the Blue Ridge were "inspiring, uplifting, and challenging" and seemed to "beckon to higher things." Over the course of time, her gifted mind and spirit touched many lives and many areas of life. She reached out to individual people, meeting them where they were, and showing them where they could go, if they put their mind to it. One of those individuals was a girl named Hepsy.

Hepsy's mother had died when she was ten, leaving her father with six children, of which Hepsy was the oldest. In spite of her many responsibilities, she never failed to attend Mary's sewing class on Thursday afternoons. On one particular day, however, she was absent.

"I don't think Hepsy's acomin' to the class anymore," a girl told Mary. "She's agoin' to git married, and they's amovin' t'other side o' the ridge."

"Married!" Mary exclaimed. "But Hepsy's only twelve years old!"

"Yes'm," the girl said. "But Hepsy'll soon be thirteen, and as soon as you're turned thirteen you're agoin' into fourteen and can git married."

Mary was dismayed. It was not unusual to see mountain girls fourteen and fifteen years old married to boys of sixteen and seventeen, but the outcomes were often disastrous. The death toll of newborn babies was high, and many little-girl wives died in childbirth. Others grew old before their time. Mary was especially upset about Hepsy, because she knew the girl wanted to continue her education.

> The man they told me she was planning to marry, I knew, was more than twice her age and a drunkard and moonshiner. Hepsy was such a promising child, by all means the brightest one in my little sewing class. . . . And now she was about to throw away every chance by marrying this no-good. It nearly broke my heart.

As she gazed across the massive hills of the Blue Ridge, draped in spring's brightest shades of yellow, pink, and purple, Mary knew she had to help Hepsy. She told Hepsy's father that his daughter deserved a chance at something better, and he agreed. Unfortunately, no matter how supportive he was, he could not afford to send Hepsy away to school.

Mary Sloop sprung into action. She wrote to friends, asking for contributions to pay Hepsy's expenses at a preparatory school in Banner Elk, about thirty miles from Crossnore. Hepsy would need clothes, too, so Mary wrote a letter to her cousins, who were about Hepsy's size, asking them to send some of their old clothes. Mary had known these two women when she was a girl, and they had always worn pretty dresses. She smiled when she pictured Hepsy in such nice things. When the wagon arrived bearing the cousins' trunk, Mary could hardly contain her excitement.

> I ran back out to the porch, opened the trunk, lifted the lid. And every dress was black! The cousins had apparently been in mourning, and had done it thoroughly. I took out black dress after black dress, and finally lifted out a bonnet with a crepe veil on it. My heart broke. The tears came. I put my head down on top of the little trunk. An old woman came up unnoticed and saw me. Directly, she touched my shoulder and inquired, her voice warm with sympathy, "Mis' Sloops, what's the matter? Is yo' folks dead?" "No," I said, "but somebody else's are." Then I explained.

At first, the woman was silent. Then she remarked that she wished the dresses were her size, because she would love to buy one of them. Mary stopped crying, hung the dresses on her front porch, and passed the word.

"Suddenly, the whole valley was in mourning!" she recalled in *Miracle in the Hills.*

Mary took the money from the sale of the black dresses, bought fabric, and made Hepsy the clothes she needed to go away to school.

When Mary first arrived in Crossnore, children attended school in the town's church. It was a dark, gloomy log building containing homemade desks "of crudest design and construction." Budding pocketknife artists had carved their initials and anything else they could think of into the wood. Many of the children did not attend school at all, and those who did were taught by well-meaning young people who had only finished a few grades themselves.

Mary's campaign to enroll all children in school resulted in increased attendance which qualified the community for two trained teachers supplied by the State Board of Education. A new school-house was built, and soon it overflowed with students. Additional rooms were added.

Eventually, a high school was built as well, but attendance was poor because many students had to travel long distances over bad roads to reach the school. Mary found a way, "through work and prayer," to provide dormitories at the high school. The Crossnore School was born.

Under Mary's guidance, the Crossnore School developed into a boarding school and was sanctioned by the Daughters of the American Revolution in 1924. Winifred Kirkland, who visited Crossnore in 1925, called Dr. Sloop "A Hundred-Horse-Power Woman." She wrote, "I have been spending a week with a mountain torrent. The humorous flow of her speech is with me still—a torrent delightedly harnessed to turn a dozen wheels, and delighted to show you those wheels in motion."

In 1928, a small hospital opened its doors in Crossnore, due largely to the Sloops' efforts and a start-up gift of $5,000 that arrived unexpectedly in the mail one day. More than ten years earlier, Eustace had brought electricity to the town by means of an outdated 2,300-pound dynamo and a dam built across the Linville River. For the most part, the days of performing surgery by kerosene lamp or outdoors under an apple tree were truly over.

Although Crossnore School began as a public institution, by 1939 it had emerged as a special place for "orphan, half-orphan, and deserted children" and "children with both parents living but without the means of procuring a High School or Vocational Education."

In her book *The Suitcases*, Anne Hall Whitt, who attended the Crossnore School from 1944 to 1950, describes her first encounter with Dr. Mary Martin Sloop: "Her hair was a cloud of white, and the lines in her face deepened in the most beautiful way as she greeted each child with a smile. Her dark blue dress with its lace collar hung loosely on her stout body, and her glasses kept slipping down her nose."

Later, Anne wrote:

> Mrs. Sloop had the courage to stand before awesome philanthropic groups asking their support for her school, but she also had the sensitivity to see into the heart of a first-grader who had been abandoned by his parents. From the day that she found a way to educate Hepsy until her death in 1962, she spent her life ministering to children. No one was too poor or too ignorant to go to her school.

Jackie Tallent, a student at Crossnore from 1942 to 1954, remembers Mrs. Sloop clearly, dressed in "long, stylish, dark-colored dresses with pleats, and always a cape—gray, black, or checkered," a big-boned woman who resembled Eleanor Roosevelt. In fact, Jackie recalls that when she first saw a photograph of Mrs. Roosevelt, she asked a schoolmate what Mrs. Sloop was doing in that picture with the President.

By this time, the Sloops' daughter, Emma, had become Emma Sloop Fink, M.D., and son Will had become a dentist. Both had returned to Crossnore to work with their parents in the town they knew and loved. Their skills were put to good use.

"In 1947, during the polio epidemic, we managed to get enough vaccine for the children," Emma recalls. "We vaccinated 3,000 in one afternoon. Today, you'd never get that many to come but people were scared."

At the age of seventy-eight, the "Grand Lady of the Blue Ridge," as Dr. Mary Martin Sloop had come to be called, received national recognition for her work with the mountain children. The Golden Rule Foundation, an organization devoted to the welfare of mothers and children, named her the "American Mother of 1951." The citation described Mary as a "doctor of medicine, a selfless citizen, an untiring crusader, teacher, religious leader, a good and great woman, and, above all, a mother whose love for children extends beyond her own flesh and blood to encompass thousands of needy youngsters."

Dr. Mary T. Martin Sloop's work did not end in 1951, or even in 1962 when she passed away. Today, Crossnore School continues to offer a "shelter from the storms" for children of the mountains and foothills who are not able to live at home. Cottages, a day school, chapel, gymnasium, dining hall, and other facilities comprise the seventy-two-acre campus. Sloop Memorial Hospital is now part of a health care network that serves all of western North Carolina.

To Dr. Mary Sloop, death held no threat. In the conclusion to *Miracle in the Hills*, LeGette Blythe recounted Mary's words:

> For me the calendar says—the calendar, mind you, and not I—that I must now be entering the uncharted maze of days along the highest slope of the last mountain. And below it there'll be the shadows of the farthest cove. But little that matters. Beyond the cove—and this I know—I shall shortly walk out into the unending Sunshine. There, I trust, I shall quickly find work to do.

Dr. Mary T. Martin Sloop is buried beside her beloved "Doctor" in the cemetery adjoining the Crossnore Presbyterian Church.❖

CHARLOTTE HAWKINS BROWN

1883–1961

First Lady of Social Graces

"*I* can pay you three dollars and fifty cents a week," the woman said.

Lottie Hawkins did some quick mental arithmetic then took the job. It was good money for babysitting just two hours a day. Now she could help her parents pay for the organdy and silk she needed to make her high school graduation outfit. When she took her place with the other members of the Class of 1900, her dress and demeanor would be in keeping with the importance of the occasion.

Spring had finally arrived in Cambridge, Massachusetts, and Lottie could almost feel her future unfolding as the dogwood and crabapple trees began to blossom. Standing just inside the door of a brand new century, she was certain her life had a purpose, and she was determined to make her mark on the world.

She had already taken a few steps in the right direction. As early as age three, she had memorized a Bible verse and recited it in church. When she was twelve, she saw the need for a Sunday School kindergarten class so she organized one herself. Just before turning fourteen, she was chosen as orator for an important church celebration. In the audience sat the governor of Massachusetts and several members of his advisory council. The group responded to Lottie's speech with enthusiastic applause, and one of the advisory council members remarked, "I expect to hear from that girl in the future."

Lottie was willing to guarantee that he would. A descendant of slaves, she knew she had opportunities her grandparents never even imagined. Still, she had a few hurdles to clear—and not just because of her race. For one thing, Lottie stood just under five feet tall. No matter how mature she was, she would have to work extra hard to convince people that she was not a child. Another concern she had was her name. A person called "Lottie" would forever be thought of as a little girl. From now on, Lottie decided, she would be known as Charlotte Eugenia Hawkins. She had already told her school principal to put that name on her diploma.

As Lottie (now Charlotte) prepared to take her tiny charge for a walk in his baby carriage, she glanced out the window. The last traces of snow had melted. Pink and white azalea buds had popped out as temperatures rose into the high fifties.

Sometimes, especially in winter, Charlotte wished she lived in North Carolina, where she had been born. Whenever she traveled to Guilford County with her mother, they always visited the old home place in Henderson. With its four columns standing straight and proud on the front porch, the house had great dignity and character. In Charlotte's mind, it represented traits she knew she possessed. She wanted others to notice those qualities in her.

Even though she liked visiting North Carolina, she understood why her family had moved to New England in 1888. Slavery had been abolished, but there still weren't many opportunities for colored people in the South. Things were different in Massachusetts. In fact, just last year the Agassiz School in Cambridge had appointed a Negro headmaster, Maria Baldwin.

Charlotte grabbed one of her school books and pushed the

Charlotte Hawkins Brown

NORTH CAROLINA DIVISION OF ARCHIVES AND HISTORY

baby buggy out the door. She liked to read as she walked, holding a book in one hand and guiding the carriage with the other. Soon, her mind was deeply engrossed in the poetry of Virgil.

"Excuse me," said a voice.

Startled, Charlotte stopped walking and looked up from her book. Before her stood a tall, middle-aged white woman with dark chestnut hair. Her stylish black dress and dignified manner did not escape Charlotte's keen eye for quality.

"I noticed you're reading Virgil. Are you a senior?"

"Yes, I am."

"In which of the schools?"

"The English School."

The woman asked several more questions, then smiled and went on her way. A few days later, Charlotte's high school principal called her into his office. He told her that Alice Freeman Palmer, renowned educator and first woman president of Wellesley College, had asked him about a "little brown-skinned girl" she had seen wheeling a baby carriage near the school.

"I told her it must be you, Lottie," he said. "Miss Deering had already mentioned to me that you were working in the afternoon."

Charlotte was not surprised that the woman who had spoken to her was highly respectable and influential. The surprise came later, after graduation, when she opened the catalog she had requested from the State Normal School at Salem. There, on the first page, Alice Freeman Palmer was listed as a member of the board of education of the state of Massachusetts, the body that governed state normal schools.

Audentis Fortuna iuvat.
Fortune assists the bold.
Virgil, *Aeneid*, Book 10, 1.284

Charlotte wrote to Mrs. Palmer, describing herself as "the little brown-skinned girl" she had seen wheeling a baby carriage and reading Virgil. In just a few days, a response arrived. Mrs. Palmer offered to cover all Charlotte's expenses at the State Normal School of her choosing. Charlotte enrolled at Salem as a member of the Class of 1902.

But Charlotte Eugenia Hawkins was not destined to remain a student for that long. In 1901, she learned of a great need for teachers in mission schools in North Carolina. As a representative from the American Missionary Association told her about Bethany Institute in Guilford County, Charlotte began to get a clearer sense of what her life's purpose was to be. She would improve education and open doors to new opportunities for her race. It seemed especially fitting to her that her life's work would begin in North Carolina, where she had taken her first breath.

In October of 1901, eighteen-year-old Charlotte Eugenia Hawkins stepped off the train in Greensboro. Already, she had begun to imagine herself in front of a classroom, sharing her love of learning with eager young students. She could almost hear the sound of her voice as she read to them from Virgil. But first, she had to get to Sedalia, and daydreaming would not accomplish that. Her letter of directions stated that she was to take the train from Greensboro to McLeansville.

"McLeansville?" said the porter at the Greensboro station. "Well, there's hardly any such thing. But the conductor might stop the train there if you keep reminding him."

Undaunted, Charlotte climbed aboard. At McLeansville, she was greeted by sturdy oaks, their leaves brilliant with autumn color, and giant pine trees, ever green. In their midst stood a small, unpainted house that was considerably less majestic. Although the building seemed unlikely to contain anything of value, it turned out to be the country store and post office for the area. Bethany Institute, she was informed, was four and one-half miles away. She set out walking and finished the journey bumping along on a wagon pulled by a mule.

Charlotte had thought the McLeansville post office was in sad shape, but that was before she saw the crude building that served as Sedalia's church and schoolroom combined. Broken plaster and missing windowpanes told a story of neglect. Fifty or sixty unkempt, barefoot children sat on homemade log seats. The words forlorn and forsaken leaped into Charlotte's mind. But then she looked into her new students' bright, questioning eyes. Suddenly, their future was all that mattered. Her life's work had truly begun.

And work she did. Although her upbringing had not prepared her for the level of poverty and hardship she encountered, she forged ahead. In addition to teaching, she organized groups and clubs in her community. Often, a portion of her meager salary went to buy clothing or supplies for her students. It seemed to Charlotte that things could not get any more dismal for the town of Sedalia, but she was wrong. In 1902, the American Missionary Association decided to close the Bethany Institute, seemingly slamming the door on all Charlotte's hopes for the bright-eyed children she had come to love. Many of the townspeople assured her that they wanted her to stay, but they were equally forthcoming about their inability to pay her.

To Charlotte Eugenia Hawkins, the solution was clear. Another school must be opened. It would incorporate the best traits of the schools she had attended in New England and offer a practical industrial education as well. She was certain she could bring the idea to life, if only she could get others to help. In June, Charlotte paid a visit to Alice Freeman Palmer in Cambridge. Mrs. Palmer was receptive and offered to approach some of her friends about funding as soon as she came back from Europe in the fall.

That was all Charlotte needed to hear. Filled with enthusiasm, she set about raising money to get the project started. It was a tall order for a girl who had just turned nineteen, but as usual, Charlotte rose to the challenge. Like a diminutive tornado, she whirled through town stirring up interest in her school. By October of 1902, a Sedalia blacksmith's shop had been converted into a day and boarding school, complete with two teachers and several female students.

Although Charlotte received much support for her school, she also encountered suspicion and disapproval. Some of the white people in the Sedalia area were concerned that this northern-educated woman would fill the students' minds with inappropriate notions of social equality. The result, they asserted, could only be hatred and racial tension. Still, Charlotte persevered, employing all possible tact and grace when dealing with her opponents. She could hardly wait to tell Mrs. Palmer what had already been accomplished.

Unfortunately, she was not to see her benefactress again. While still overseas, Mrs. Palmer became seriously ill and died in a Paris hospital. It was a harsh blow for Charlotte personally and professionally, yet she could not give up. Knowing that her friend had understood and shared her vision, she christened her school The Alice Freeman Palmer Memorial Institute. Later, the institute became known simply as Palmer or PMI.

Hos successus alit: possunt, quia posse videntur.
These success encourages: they can because they think they can.
Virgil, *Aeneid*, Book 5, I.231

Over the next forty years, Charlotte's efforts brought PMI to the attention of national figures such as Booker T. Washington, Harvard University President Charles William Eliot, and Boston philanthropists Carrie and Galen Stone. As if her tireless work on behalf of PMI were not enough, she also threw herself into community and church activities. She was one of the organizers and founders of the North Carolina State Federation of Negro Women's Clubs—part of a national organization committed to the betterment of Negro womanhood.

Keenly interested in racial harmony, Charlotte was involved in numerous efforts to improve race relations in the South. Initially, she took a conservative approach, often tolerating behavior she could neither understand nor condone.

One of her most traumatic experiences occurred in 1920 while she was en route to a women's interracial meeting in Memphis. She had looked forward to the conference, the purpose of which was to "make the Negro woman unashamed and unafraid." After spending the night in a berth on the train, she started to take a seat in the coach for the rest of the journey. A group of white men intercepted her and forcibly "escorted" her to the Negro coach, marching her through three cars containing white women on their way to the same conference.

In general, Charlotte met this type of personal humiliation with her head held high, emulating the example set by Booker T. Washington and others. In the halls of Palmer, she placed signs that read "Move Quietly. Speak Softly." However, as black Americans trooped into Europe along with their white comrades to fight in World War II, she was unable to conceal her outrage at the continuing inequality on the home front. Sandra N. Smith and Earle H. West of Howard University described her response to this injustice in an article for *The Journal of Negro Education* published in 1982.

> In bitterly eloquent words, she called for no more delay in granting to all citizens the freedoms for which blacks were being asked to sacrifice their lives. . . . In a New York address, she bluntly stated that the refusal to "open the doors of labor to black citizens" was exhibiting "the very Hitlerism you are seeking to destroy." There would be no

lasting peace, she prophesied, "so long as the white race seeks to deprive the darker people of the world of their God-given rights to live, to work, to have the education, the leisure, the culture that they covet for themselves."

Although Charlotte excelled in nearly everything she attempted, her marriage to Harvard graduate Edward S. Brown in 1911 lasted only a year. Some have speculated that the difficulties they faced in their relationship stemmed from the very traits that made Charlotte successful in the vast majority of her endeavors.

"Charlotte Hawkins Brown was not a modest person," confides Ruth Totton, whose mother, Ethel, was one of Charlotte's close friends. "She was very aware of her achievements. In May of 1946, while she was in Boston, she found out I had just graduated from college. She called and we talked for awhile. When she learned that I didn't yet have a job, she told me to take a pen and write 'Dear Dr. Brown, I have just graduated from Fisk University with a degree in physical education and I'm interested in teaching at your school. . . .' She dictated the whole letter and told me to mail it to Palmer!"

Ruth did as she was told but as the weeks passed, she heard nothing from PMI. Meanwhile, Boston University accepted her as a graduate student, and she made plans to attend.

"In August, I received a message to call Dr. Brown," Ruth recalls. "She said, 'I'm calling to let you know you got the job. I will expect you the day after Labor Day. Let me know which train you are taking and I will send my car for you. Give your mother my best.' We had not discussed salary or the subjects I would teach or any of those details!"

Nevertheless, Ruth reported for duty as summoned. She admired Dr. Brown and wanted to work with her. Ruth and another young woman, Charlotte's secretary, lived with Charlotte in her house in Sedalia.

"Some people were afraid of her," Ruth says.

But she meant to generate respect, not fear. She needed people to do things her way. Imagine coming down to the segregated South in 1902, having been raised in New England. I think she felt the only way she could accomplish anything at all was to hold people in check and control them.

Living in her home, we saw a side of her that others didn't often see. She was a very kind, concerned person. Her whole life was that school and the children. She never turned anyone down. But she taught them to earn their way. Everyone had chores to do, not just the students who were there on scholarship. She made sure people were treated equally.

In the November 1930 issue of *Abbott's Monthly*, Lucinda Yancey Saunders wrote of Charlotte Hawkins Brown:

Mrs. Brown has been a social worker in the truest sense of the word, for she has ministered to every kind of need in the community from going in the night to help with a sick child or baby to conducting religious service in the pulpit on Sunday. She has taught the people to buy their farms on the co-operative plan, and the beauty and neatness and thrift of the homes and farms in the community, as well as the prosperity, all bear silent witness to the service Charlotte Hawkins Brown has rendered at Sedalia.

From its beginning as a small elementary school for neighborhood children, PMI grew into a facility that offered college preparatory classes in a high school setting. Eventually, it became a junior college serving middle- and upper-class boys and girls from many states as well as Africa, Bermuda, Central America, and Cuba. Math, literature, languages, music, drama, and art were taught. In addition, PMI was the only high school in North Carolina to offer African-American history. These academic subjects were presented as only part of a complete education.

Charlotte's mother and grandmother had imparted to her an appreciation of beauty and refinement. She was certain that an emphasis on culture would "usher in better days" for her people. As she explained in her book *The Correct Thing to Do, to Say, to Wear*: "The cultivation of traits of honor, thoughtfulness, politeness, honesty, order, and proper appreciation of values is just as much a part of education as is the storing up in one's mind of a vast accumulation of historic, mathematical, and scientific facts."

In *The Correct Thing*, Charlotte detailed appropriate behavior for men and women in every area of life, including home, school, church, dances, concerts, and travel. She made countless public appearances to encourage politeness and consideration of others. Her devotion to decorum moved Eleanor Roosevelt to dub her "First Lady of Social Graces."

Charlotte's own deep religious faith was another cornerstone of PMI, as reflected in the Palmer Prayer: "Dear God, help me to take Jesus in earnest, to believe the things that he said, and to put these things to the test in my everyday life."

Her emphasis on "education, religion, and culture" earned her a place as one of the "Three Bs of Education," together with African-American educators Mary McLeod Bethune and Nannie Helen Burroughs. Bethune's triangle of ideas and lessons included "the head, the heart, and the hand." For Burroughs, the triangle consisted of "the book, the Bible, and the broom."

Charlotte's friendship with Mary McLeod Bethune extended beyond academics into the realm of *haute couture*. "Dr. Brown would despair at Mary McLeod Bethune's choice of outfits," Ruth Totton says. "She would call her up to tell her a particular dress 'didn't do a thing for her.' When Mary was on the cover of *Ebony* magazine, all Dr. Brown could say was 'Where did she get that hat?'"

Although Charlotte's input was never requested by top fashion designers, her accomplishments did earn her honorary degrees from many institutions of higher learning. North Carolina Central University in Durham conferred upon her an honorary masters degree. From Howard University in Washington, D.C., she received an honorary doctorate. During her life, she was awarded a total of seven honorary degrees.

Up until the very day she retired in 1952, Charlotte was on a fast track, always pushing ahead. "The Dynamo," as her colleagues called her, was not a morning person or a night person.

"She was an 'all day and half the night person,'" Ruth says.

She would get in at midnight or one o'clock after taking the night train from a speaking engagement. Instead of crawling into bed like most people would, she wanted to tell us everything that had happened on her trip. We had to be up to greet her with the lights on. There we would sit in the middle of the night, eating finger sandwiches and cookies and listening to anecdotes.

Unfortunately, Charlotte's selfless devotion to so many worthwhile projects caused her to neglect her own health. "She didn't take care of herself," Ruth says. "I really feel that contributed to an early death."

In later life, Charlotte Hawkins Brown suffered from diabetes and from a condition now known as Alzheimer's Disease. At the age of seventy-seven, following an extended illness, she died at Memorial Hospital in Greensboro, North Carolina.

Although PMI's doors closed to students in 1971, Charlotte's dream lives on. In 1987, the state of North Carolina opened the former Palmer Institute in Sedalia as a memorial to African-American education and women's history in North Carolina. Equally alive is the legacy handed down by Palmer's more than one thousand graduates and the hundreds of thousands who heard Charlotte speak for racial justice. The bright eyes of their children's children reflect the spirit of a little girl named Lottie and the words of the poet Virgil:

Macte nova virtute, puer, sic itur ad astra.
Blessings on your young courage, boy; that's the way to the stars.
Virgil, *Aeneid*, Book 9, 1.641❖

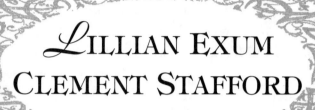

LILLIAN EXUM CLEMENT STAFFORD
1894–1925

The Lady They Called "Brother Exum"

*R*ain pattered gently on the roof and windows of the Clement house on Hollywood Street in Asheville, North Carolina. A misty fog had settled over the Blue Ridge Mountains surrounding the quiet community. In the distance, thunder rumbled and rolled.

Before the 1880s, Asheville had been a town of 2,610 inhabitants. By 1900, the arrival of the railroad had transformed it into a city of almost 15,000. The new decade promised even more growth, but the Blue Ridge and Smoky Mountains still stood wild and proud, as they had for centuries, unimpressed with what human beings called "progress."

Inside the house on Hollywood, Lillian Exum Clement, her four brothers, and three sisters passed the time by paging through an encyclopedia, pointing out people or places that best illustrated their life's dreams. The oldest sister, Bertha, made her way to "N" for Florence Nightingale, a woman she greatly admired. Brother Latta, who loved gardening, turned to "B." He was deeply impressed by Luther Burbank's greenhouse in California.

Lillian Exum Clement

NORTH CAROLINA DIVISION OF ARCHIVES AND HISTORY

Next came Lillian Exum's turn. A pretty, dark-haired girl, she wore the frills and lace popular in her day. The name Lillian seemed to suit her feminine appearance perfectly. However, she answered to her middle name, "Exum" or sometimes just "Ex." Quickly, she flipped the pages of the encyclopedia until she arrived at a speech from Shakespeare's *Merchant of Venice*.

The scene was a court of justice. The speaker was an intelligent, quick-witted woman named Portia. Portia had dressed as a lawyer in order to plead the case of Antonio, who was doomed to suffer severe, though seemingly just, treatment.

"The quality of mercy is not strain'd," Exum began in her melodic voice. "It droppeth as the gentle rain from heaven Upon the place beneath: it is twice blest."

From time to time, a clap of thunder provided punctuation as she continued to read:

> It blesseth him that gives and him that takes:
> 'Tis mightiest in the mightiest: it becomes
> The throned monarch better than his crown;
> His sceptre shows the force of temporal power,
> The attribute to awe and majesty,
> Wherein doth sit the dread and fear of kings;
> But mercy is above this sceptred sway;
> It is enthroned in the hearts of kings,
> It is an attribute to God himself;
> And earthly power doth then show likest God's
> When mercy seasons justice.

Portia's courtroom words won Antonio's case, and when Exum Clement recited the famous speech, she foreshadowed her own future with uncanny accuracy. It was to be a long road and not without hazard.

Lillian Exum Clement was born in March 1894 in the mountains of western North Carolina, as the stern winds of winter began to yield to spring's mirth. The sixth child of George Washington Clement and Sarah Elizabeth Burnette Clement, Exum learned her ABCs in a one-room schoolhouse. Her father was the son of a planter whose plantation had been destroyed in the War Between the States. He worked for the railroad in the town of Black Mountain. Her mother's family had settled the North Fork of Black Mountain when it was still Indian Country.

When Exum was about thirteen, her father was hired to help build George Vanderbilt's four-story mansion in Asheville. Vanderbilt was heir to his family's steam shipping and railroad fortune and had come to North Carolina to create "a fine private mansion in the most beautiful place in the world."

Included in the land Vanderbilt purchased was the small town of Best on the Swannanoa River. Vanderbilt had the existing buildings torn down and constructed a village of English style cottages. This "ideal community" housed the Clements and others who worked on the Vanderbilt estate.

Biltmore Village, as it was named, boasted not only homes, but a school, hospital, and house of worship. The early Gothic-style All Soul's Episcopal Church, located in the heart of Biltmore, was the scene of Exum's confirmation into the Christian faith. For the ceremony, she wore an exquisite full-length white dress with a high neck, trimmed in handmade lace. Special touches, like the tiny decorative buttons from waist to neck and a subtle pattern of squares in the material, completed the picture of genteel southern femininity. Her delicate beauty belied the will of iron within.

Exum Clement graduated from All Soul's Parish School, staffed by a corps of instructors from the Teachers' College of Columbia University. She then attended the Normal and Collegiate Institute and Asheville Business College. In today's world, she would most likely have proceeded to law school. In the early 1900s, however, there were no woman lawyers. Exum would have to follow a different route to realize her dream. Her first step was to take a job as a secretary for the sheriff's office. By day, she typed, filed, and took dictation. At night, she attended classes taught by practicing attorneys J. J. Britt and Robert C. Goldstein. Exum studied long after most of the city was asleep, then sank into bed, exhausted, only to get up and start all over again the next morning.

Encouraging Exum in her lofty goal was Edith Vanderbilt, George's wife, who had taken a liking to the bright, young woman. Exum also made a lasting impression on Goldstein, who was quoted by the *Asheville Citizen* as saying:

> She has an unusual legal mind, being very capable, thorough and systematic in all the courses and has never missed a class or varied in her time of reporting for work one minute during the time she was a member of my class. She is not only familiar with the principles of law, but with its history and philosophy as well.

On February 7, 1916, Exum Clement sat for the North Carolina bar exam. Most of the seventy men who joined her had the advantage of a university education. Nevertheless, Exum not only passed, she received one of the prizes offered for the highest grades.

Thus, at the ripe old age of twenty-two, she graciously accepted a bouquet of carnations from Judge Thomas A. Jones and took her oath before Judge W. F. Harding. One could easily imagine the spirit of Shakespeare's Portia smiling upon her "sister," Buncombe County's first female attorney. During the ceremony, Judge Jones referred to Miss Clement by the nickname that would forever be hers alone: "Brother Exum."

No doubt Portia would also have cheered as Exum hung out

her shingle in downtown Asheville, becoming North Carolina's first woman lawyer without male partners. Women of today's generation may bemoan the "glass ceiling," but in 1917, Exum stood in a glass enclosure, on display while men watched and waited for her to prove to them she was capable. She succeeded, although some took more convincing than others.

The *Greensboro Daily News* publicized her story of a handsome, dark, Italian man with glittering white teeth who arrived at her law office, demanding to see "the lawyer of the place."

"But this is my office—I am the lawyer," Exum explained.

"Oh, no! You're not a lawyer. You just work for a lawyer," he stated.

The look on his face was too comical for words when he finally understood that she was, indeed, "the boss of the shop."

"Brother Exum" quickly built a reputation as a shrewd and competent criminal lawyer. So capable was she that in 1920, the leaders of the Democratic Party in her state approached her to run for Buncombe County representative to the State Legislature. She accepted their nomination.

Meanwhile, a storm was sweeping across America. Like a tornado, the women's suffrage movement touched down in every state from California to Maine. In North Carolina, a bill giving women the vote had been introduced as early as 1897, to no avail.

"Brother Exum" did not agitate with throngs of protesters or make impassioned speeches about suffrage. While women all over the country paraded and postured, she stepped unobtrusively yet firmly into the future. When the votes for Buncombe County representative were tallied, Exum had won, and in no small way. She beat her male opponent by a margin of 10,368 to 41. It was the largest majority ever polled in the state up to that time.

Exum's daughter, Stafford Anders, sums up her mother's point of view on the suffrage issue: "Mother didn't have much patience with the way some of the suffragettes behaved. She knew change was needed, but she believed that she could accomplish more by being quiet and feminine and having men eat out of her hand, which they did."

On August 26, 1920, the Nineteenth Amendment was passed, guaranteeing every woman the right to vote and in 1921, L. Exum Clement took the oath of office to become the first female legislator in North Carolina. Slender, with her large, dark eyes, she was as beautiful as she was intelligent. An article in the *Greensboro Daily News* dated January 15, 1921, offered this description: "Small in stature, modest and retiring in manner, unassuming but keenly alert to situations requiring clearness of thought, she is all that the most exacting would demand. . . . She wears a Norfolk jacket of green tweed with a small velvet hat, and in her modest attire is as little conspicuous as any other member of the house."

When Stafford Anders was very young, she saw an official portrait of her mother and the other legislators. She recalls:

They were a stern-looking bunch, with long beards and frowning faces. I had heard Mother described as "beautiful," but the woman in the picture wore unflattering glasses, a brimmed hat, and an expression as grim as that of the men. Finally, I realized Mother was doing her best to seem older than her twenty-seven years, worthy of the high post entrusted to her. It was the best she could do— short of growing a beard!

Of her experience running for office, Exum said:

I was afraid at first that men would oppose me because I am a woman, but I don't feel that way now. I have always worked with men, and I know them as they are. I have no false illusions or fears of them. . . . I am by nature very conservative, but I am firm in my convictions. I want to blaze a trail for other women. I know that years from now there will be many other women in politics, but you have to start a thing.

And start it she did.

Within one week of being sworn in, the Honorable Exum introduced her first bill—to prohibit railroads from hiring illiterates as foremen, brakemen, and flagmen.

Taking pity on women who had been deserted by their husbands, she next introduced a bill that amended legislation so divorce could be attained after five years of abandonment instead of ten. She also introduced what became known as the Clement Bill, a measure calling for private voting booths and a secret ballot. It seemed obvious to her that this was the only democratic way to elect one's leaders. Her "Pure Milk Bill," which called for tuberculin testing of dairy cattle and sanitary dairy barns, garnered the praise of physicians and health authorities across the state. In all, she introduced seventeen bills, sixteen of which became laws.

Not everyone joined in high praise of "Brother Exum," however.

"You Jezebel!" a woman yelled at her as she sat quietly at a political meeting, and once, a man who disagreed with her viewpoint attacked her, breaking her nose.

On another occasion, she faced a less-than-hospitable crowd for the sake of a cause dear to her heart. The Lindley Home was a refuge for unwed mothers and delinquent girls in Exum's native Buncombe County. It was her dream to bring state control and support money to the home which had been operated as a private welfare institution for thirty years. Its director, Mrs. Hilliard, was retiring due to advanced age. At a rally, Exum stepped forward to plead for a compassionate, realistic approach to the predicament of troubled women and girls. Exum believed it was not a problem that could be solved by shutting the door on people like those who lived at The Lindley Home

She knew it was a touchy subject. She was well aware that to some, her proposal represented a reward for wrongdoing and undeserved support for "questionable young women." Even so, she was taken by surprise when opponents in the crowd began to throw eggs and overripe vegetables at her. The accusations and condemnations they hurled were even more hurtful, but she rose above their attack. Brushing her spattered clothes, she patiently waited for them to grow quiet, much as a kindergarten teacher gets the attention of her students by falling silent. Finally, she spoke with characteristic dignity and grace. "Tonight, I am reminded of a time long ago by a city gate, when the weapons of the people, who had passed judgment on a woman, were not eggs but hard stones. It is not for you nor me to condemn nor to cast the first stone. Rather to render aid to the unfortunate so they may also go their way and sin no more."

To Exum's relief, The Lindley Home did not have to close its doors. Under the auspices of the State of North Carolina, it continued its charitable work long after she herself passed from this life.

All in all, the words and gestures of support she received from North Carolinians far outweighed any damage she incurred at their hands. In so many ways, she and her constituents, especially those from Asheville, were like family. Together, in 1912, they had marveled when Edwin Wiley Grove of St. Louis bought Sunset Mountain and proceeded to build a massive, grand hotel out of solid granite. Side by side, they had endured the terror of the flood of 1916 that sent five feet of swirling water and mud into all corners of the city and killed six people. In 1919, when World War I ended, they cheered and hugged each other as their boys in uniform paraded down Patton Avenue under a replica of the French "Arch of Triumph."

In 1921, Exum Clement married Elias Eller Stafford in a small, quiet ceremony. A staff writer and telegraph editor for the *Asheville Citizen*, Stafford had attended Wake Forest College and lived in North Wilkesboro, North Carolina, before moving to Asheville.

Although the Honorable Exum did not run for public office again, she was appointed by Governor Morrison to the position of director of the State Hospital of Morganton. She was also one of the founders of the Asheville Business and Professional Women's Club.

In addition, Exum served as registrar of a chapter of the United Daughters of the Confederacy named for another remarkable North Carolina woman, Fanny Patton. Like Exum, "Miss Fanny" belonged to one of the Asheville area's pioneering families. As one of the Ladies of the Flower Mission, Fanny was a co-founder of Asheville Mission Hospital, which opened its doors in 1885. She passed away in 1918, having served her community faithfully as a historian, philanthropist, health care champion, and church worker.

Like Fanny Patton, Exum Clement was committed to relieving suffering and distress. Stafford Anders tells of an incident which illustrated her mother's gift for translating beliefs into action:

> One day, Mother looked out the back window of her Asheville law office and saw a young woman sitting on a park bench. Several days passed, and the woman reappeared each day. Finally, Mother approached her and asked if she needed help. The girl, whose name was Rebecca, burst into tears. Between sobs, she told Mother that she had come into town from the mountains to work as a domestic for a wealthy family. Her employer's son had seduced her, and when his parents found out she was preg-

nant, they dismissed her. Her own family threw her out when they learned of her shameful condition. She had nowhere to go. Needless to say, Mother took Rebecca in. That's the way she was.

Soon, to Exum's joy, she discovered that she herself was pregnant. In the fall of 1924, the Staffords became proud parents of a baby girl. The infant was premature, weighing just four pounds.

"I was Asheville's first incubator baby," Stafford Anders declares. "My only claim to fame."

At about the same time, Rebecca also gave birth to a girl. Exum's poor health prevented her from nursing her baby, but Rebecca was able to feed both infants. It was fitting that Exum's own child was able to thrive and grow because of her mother's kindness to an outcast stranger.

Exum's delight in her tiny daughter was as great or greater than the satisfaction she received from her many previous accomplishments. As the weeks passed, however, she continued to feel weak and unwell. Determined to overcome this latest challenge, she focused her attention on her baby. Her diary entry on the day of tiny Nancy Lillian Exum Clement Stafford's birth began "You were born today." The final entry in the diary read "Last night you slept in a room beside mother's, but I can hear you calling me, and I'll always come."

To the great sorrow of loved ones, colleagues and dignitaries alike, Lillian Exum Clement Stafford died of complications from pneumonia in February of 1925, just short of her thirty-first birthday. Her baby was just twenty-one months old.

Exum Stafford's eulogy in the *Asheville Times* read, "Suffering borne with fortitude is ended and Mrs. L. Exum Clement Stafford has crossed the borders to the life beyond, leaving the memory of endearing personal qualities and a life of unusual note. A daughter of the present age, she held to the best of the old days while adopting the best of the new."

Although Stafford Anders does not remember her mother, she treasures the many stories and descriptions shared by her grandparents and her Aunt Nancy Rebecca, who raised her, as well as the many physical mementos in her possession.

The Clement children's encyclopedia games proved to be more than child's play. Bertha, who admired Florence Nightingale, became a nurse and head of the Anti-Tuberculosis Association of Alabama. Latta, lover of gardening, became a horticulturist. Exum, the pretty girl with dark, glossy braids, became a lawyer—and more than that, the embodiment of Portia's words:

> But mercy is above this sceptred sway;
> It is enthroned in the hearts of kings,
> It is an attribute to God himself;
> And earthly power doth then show likest God's
> When mercy seasons justice.✤

Maggie Axe Wachacha
1894–1993

Healer, Teacher, and Beloved Woman

The mountains, huge and hulking, rose into ash-gray skies. Veiled in fog, their dark shapes all but disappeared in places, then revealed themselves through breaks in the smoky haze. These wild hills, thick with forests, lay hunched in the deep sleep of winter. Along the ridges, barren tree trunks reached stark and sharp into the clouded sky like quills from the backs of porcupines. Soon, when spring arrived, rushing rivers and singing creeks would tumble through the gorge. Small waterfalls would splash over the rocks and large ones would roar. But for now, the waters moved sluggishly, or lay still against the frozen ground.

The mountains bore the name Sha-cona-ge—land of the blue mist or blue smoke. The names of individual peaks were equally proud—Tu-ti, Unaka, Tsiya-hi. According to Cherokee legend, these hills and valleys had been formed by the wings of the Great Buzzard as he skimmed the surface of the wet earth long ago, when the world was new. The white people called this place "North Carolina's last frontier," and they called the mountains the Appalachians, the Smokies, or the Blue Ridge.

MAGGIE AXE WACHACHA

Maggie Axe Wachacha

COURTESY: WILMA MILLSAPS

On the crest of one peak, almost hidden by fog, stood a line of horses. Their riders sat tall, watching and waiting. The snow-laden branches of the pine and cedar swayed, and the cold wind seemed to murmur the names of the seven Cherokee clans: Ani'-Wa'ya, Ani'-Kawi , Ani'-Tsi'skwa, Ani'-Wa'di, Ani'-Saha'ni, Ani'-Ga'tage'wi, Ani'-Gila'hi.

Ten-year-old Maggie Axe squinted into the distance. She belonged to Ani'-Wa'ya, the Wolf Clan, largest of the seven. As she stared through the haze, the men on horseback shimmered like ghosts. She blinked, and they were gone. They had probably never been there at all, Maggie realized. She knew large bands of Cherokee no longer roamed the hills in search of game. The United States government had removed most of them to Oklahoma more than sixty years earlier, in 1838. Thousands of the men, women, and children who were forced to make the trip west died from exposure and disease. They had truly traveled a "Trail of Tears." In Maggie's village, the old ones still talked about Tsali, who escaped into the mountains but later sacrificed himself and his sons so that hundreds of others would be allowed to stay in the land of their ancestors.

Shivering, Maggie pulled her thin coat tighter around her. To her ears came a familiar sound—haunting and lonely, strangely musical, barely audible as it floated on the wind. It was a single voice, rising and dissolving into the mist. Wa'ya was calling his friends, or perhaps claiming his territory. With a smile, Maggie turned and walked a well-worn path back through the woods. The mingled aroma of bean bread and coffee greeted her as she entered the one-room log house she called home.

Maggie's ancestors were among the Cherokee who managed to remain in the mountains of North Carolina instead of being marched to Oklahoma. They considered themselves fortunate, but their lives were never the same after the removal. As anthropologist Sharlotte Neely reported in her book, *Snowbird Cherokees: People of Persistence*:

During the first two decades of the twentieth century the role of the Bureau of Indian Affairs in Cherokee schools bordered on the dictatorial. White teachers became the norm and boarding schools the ideal. Children were beaten for speaking the Cherokee language and encouraged to adopt white cultural patterns to the exclusion of those Cherokee.

The word "Cherokee" had no meaning in Maggie Axe's native language. Her people called themselves Ani´-Yun´wiya´ meaning "principal people" or "real people." Historians have determined that the name "Cherokee" was probably a corruption of "Tsa´ragi" or "Tsa´lagi," words occasionally used among the Cherokee. In historical records, "Cherokee" is spelled at least fifty different ways.

Efforts to change the culture of the Cherokee were strong during Maggie's youth. In church, she was taught that the mountains and valleys were not formed by the Great Buzzard's wings but by God. Every Sunday, she listened eagerly to stories from the Christian Bible, translated into Cherokee. Maggie loved to hear about Jesus and His love, the miracles He performed, and the sacrifice He made. She quickly memorized Christian hymns. Yet she still felt connected to many of the old ways. At the age of ten, she began learning the skills of midwifery from her aunt and the art of herbal medicine from her grandmother.

For centuries, the Cherokee had used plants to cure sickness. Revered storytellers like A'yun´ini or "Swimmer" explained to each generation the reason for this tradition. The tale was also included in *Myths of the Cherokee* published in 1901 by the Bureau of American Ethnology. The author was anthropologist James Mooney, who lived among the Cherokee during the late 1800s.

In the old days the beasts, birds, fishes, insects, and plants could all talk, and they and the people lived together in peace and friendship. But as time went on the people increased so rapidly that their settlements spread over the whole earth, and the poor animals found themselves beginning to be cramped for room. This was bad enough, but to make it worse Man invented bows, knives, blowguns, spears and hooks, and began to slaughter the larger animals, birds, and fishes for their flesh or their skins, while the smaller creatures, such as the frogs and worms, were crushed and trodden upon without thought, out of pure carelessness or contempt. So the animals resolved to consult upon measures for their common safety.

According to the legend, the animals decided the best way to control humans was to plague them with diseases.

When the Plants, who were friendly to Man, heard what had been done by the animals, they determined to defeat the latters' evil designs. Each Tree, Shrub, and Herb, down even to the Grasses and Mosses, said: "I shall appear to help Man when he calls upon me in his need." Thus came medicine; and the plants, every one of which has its use if we only knew it, furnish the remedy to counteract the evil wrought by the revengeful animals.

While learning the secrets of the medicine woman, Maggie lived where she had been born, in Snowbird Gap in Graham County. Her home was more than fifty miles from the Qualla Boundary of Swain County, where the vast majority of her tribe was located. Although the two factions of the tribe had much in common, they spoke different dialects of Cherokee.

Over the years, the main Cherokee Indian Reservation became a center for tourism, attracting thousands of visitors annually. Boxed in by the mountains, Maggie's community remained more isolated. At the same time, because Snowbird reservation lands were intermingled with white-owned lands, the Cherokee and non-Cherokee inhabitants interacted regularly.

Not much is known about Maggie's early childhood. According to tribal records, she was born to Will and Caroline Cornsilk Axe on September 16, 1894—in the Cherokee "Month of the Nut Moon." From interviews with Maggie and her family in 1991, writer Jennifer Ravi gleaned the following information:

> The language always spoken in her home was Cherokee. She taught herself to write it at home when she was seven years old, using chalk or writing in the dirt. Sometimes her father read it to her and she would write it in chalk on a slab of slate rock. Her father told her that one day she would go to Cherokee and work, and this provided an incentive to learn. She attended a one-room, English-speaking school four months out of the year, when it was either too cold to work or when there was no work to be done. She stopped attending after the fourth grade. Her English began with the words "Jesus Christ," and the rest came easily from listening to people talk.

In an interview for the *Journal of Cherokee Studies* in 1987, Maggie described some of her memories of the past to Lois Calonehuskie:

> I remember the livestock. There were about a hundred pigs when I first moved here. Now you don't see any pigs. Pigs and hogs were so fat. There were plenty of chestnuts back then. That's what they lived on. They belonged to

everybody. When we needed some meat, we just butchered one. Cows were there, too. We had a fence around the house so the cows wouldn't come in the yard. Cows were loose until they made a law that you had to fence in your stock. They couldn't roam the mountains like they did before. Many pigs, cows, and sheep went wild or got eaten up by wild animals.

Maggie's dual career as a healer and midwife blossomed as she grew older. Using the age-old formulas and incantations she learned from her grandmother, she treated everything from headaches and broken bones to gallstones and diabetes. A drink made from the ginseng root was useful against headaches and cramps. Maggie always made sure to address the root as "Little Man, Most Powerful Magician" in the fashion of Cherokee priests.

As a midwife, Maggie assisted in the delivery of more than three thousand babies. During childbirth, tea made from the inner bark of the wild black cherry was often given to mothers to relieve their pain. Maggie regularly walked great distances, day and night, no matter what the weather, to help those who needed her.

In 1935, Maggie met and married Jarrett Wachacha. Twenty years older than Maggie, Jarrett was a member of the Deer Clan, Ani´-Kawi . He was descended from Wachacha, brother of Tsunu´lahun´ski or "Junaluska." Junaluska was credited with saving Andrew Jackson's life during the Battle of Horseshoe Bend in 1814. Nevertheless, he was exiled with his people to Oklahoma. Later, he walked back to Graham County, where he was eventually granted the right of citizenship and a tract of land. He is buried in a boulder-marked grave near Robbinsville.

When Maggie and Jarrett married, Jarrett already had a son named Riley, and Maggie had a daughter named Lucinda. Riley and Lucinda later married each other. In 1936, Maggie and Jarrett's daughter, Winnona, was born. The following year, Maggie took on yet another important role—Tribal Indian Clerk for the Eastern Band of Cherokee Indians. In 1987, she explained to Lois Calonehuskie how she got the job: "The former Clerk [Will West Long] said he couldn't write any more. I'd taught myself to write in the Cherokee language. . . . Back then they held the Council meeting for two weeks once a year in the fall. The meeting lasted three days, and it was all in the Cherokee language. No English was spoken."

Annual meetings were held thirty miles away in the town of Cherokee. It took Maggie and Jarrett, who was an elected council-man from Snowbird Township, two days to walk there. Starting out at three or four o'clock in the morning, they would spend the night at a friend's house and continue early the next morning. When they had the money, they rode the midnight train instead. Maggie's du-ties included transcribing the minutes of the meetings into the Chero-kee Syllabary, the written language of the Cherokee. She held the position of Tribal Indian Clerk for more than forty years.

In addition to being a healer, midwife, and tribal clerk, Maggie was also a teacher. She taught Sunday School at Zion Hill Baptist Church and taught the Cherokee Syllabary to students in the Robbinsville school system, at Tri-County Technical College, and in the Adult Education Program of Graham County. In this way, she helped preserve a heritage and language nearly lost during the years of forced acculturation.

Bill Millsaps of Robbinsville remembers Maggie fondly.

When I was little, my dad operated a country store and the Wachachas were regular customers. At age eight, I began learning the Indian Syllabary from Maggie and the Cherokee language from the family. To this day, I read and write Cherokee with much accuracy. I must admit that I've lost my ability to speak as fluently as I would like. Maggie was a medicine lady and has doctored on many folks, me included. She was a very unique person.

Millsaps particularly enjoys telling a story about the time he was having dinner with Maggie's family at her daughter Lucinda's home. The baked ham looked and smelled delicious, but Bill had a terrible toothache and couldn't eat.

They sent me up to Maggie's house. She went behind the smokehouse and came back with some sticks. She told me to boil them, take a spoonful of the liquid, and hold it against my tooth. It worked! Later, I asked some of her family what those sticks were. They started to giggle. Finally, one of them said "The sticks don't matter. It was the words she said over them." Now, I don't know whether it makes any sense or not, but I know my toothache went away.

Conjuring, the use of magic to influence people and events, has always been part of the Cherokee tradition. Even in the days of "enlightenment" that followed the influx of whites into the area, conjuring remained a viable approach to all manner of problems. In fact, many of the most noted conjurers also served as ministers in the local churches. Sharlotte Neely, author of *Snowbird Cherokees*, heard the following explanation during a sermon at Buffalo Baptist Church: "Only Jesus can heal illness, accomplishing His purpose through physicians or 'conjure men,' whose duty it is to locate the plant or herb which will cure a particular disease."

The advances of medicine during the twentieth century have not been shunned by the Cherokee, but at times, the old remedies still seem to work the best.

In 1978, the joint council of the Western Band of Cherokee of Oklahoma and the Eastern Band of Cherokee of North Carolina bestowed upon Maggie Axe Wachacha the title of "Beloved Woman." As Gilliam (Gill) Jackson reported in *The Cherokee One Feather*, the title traditionally was granted to the widowed wife of the Principal Chief. Jackson went on to say:

> One of the most important individuals in traditional Cherokee society was a "Beloved Woman" which was an honored title of a very aged, respected female who played an important role in the most solemn ceremonies of the Cherokee people. . . . In recent time the traditional role of "Beloved Woman" . . . has been bestowed upon a modern day woman, Maggie Wachacha. . . . She also has the distinction of being the only female in Cherokee history to have a Tribal Building named in her honor. Other Tribal Buildings have been named after Tribal Chiefs and war heroes.

In 1986, *Newsweek* magazine recognized Maggie as one of one hundred American heroes. That same year, she was one of five women to receive the North Carolina Distinguished Woman Award, presented by Governor Jim Martin.

By age 97, Maggie had given up clerking, midwifery, and healing, although people still came to her for herbal treatments. Jarrett had passed away seventeen years earlier in 1974, at age 101. Maggie had come to prefer conversing in Cherokee, letting others translate to English if necessary.

Maggie's great-granddaughter, Carolyn, remembers her great-grandmother as a "happy, perky person" who made her own buttermilk butter and collected rocks shaped like familiar objects or animals. She was often seen working in her garden, sporting the red kerchief worn by many of the older Cherokee women. Her corn crib was always full.

In Maggie's final months, Carolyn often stopped by to check on her. She remembers hearing Maggie's voice singing softly in Cherokee from her bedroom. Carolyn had heard old people sing this way before. To her, it sounded like a song of parting, of preparing to leave this world. The song she remembers hearing is called "Sqwatinisesti Yihuwa" ("Guide Me, Jehovah"). The chorus of the hymn is a simple plea: "Forever, forever, guide, direct and help me. Forever, forever, guide, direct and help me."

Maggie Axe Wachacha died on February 3, 1993, in the Cherokee "Month of the Bony Moon." At her funeral, Bill Millsaps and his wife, Wilma, sang two of Maggie's favorite hymns in Cherokee: "Oonelanvhi Oowetsi" ("Amazing Grace") and "Oowoduhadi-quinassv" ("A Beautiful Life"). Maggie is buried on a hillside not far from a house where she once lived. The small, deserted structure is almost completely hidden by the wild flowers and grasses of Snowbird Gap.

Standing beside Maggie's grave, encircled by the massive mountains, it is easy to understand the fierce devotion the "principal people" felt for this land and to regret the ruling that tore so many of them away. Today, Wa´ya's soulful howl is heard but rarely in this place. Yet sometimes ghostly men on horseback still appear along the highest ridge. They speak only Cherokee. They live close to the earth that was shaped by Great Buzzard's wings. And they will never be removed.✤

BIBLIOGRAPHY

GENERAL REFERENCES

Ashe, Samuel A., ed. *Biographical History of North Carolina*, 8 vols. Greensboro, NC: Charles L. Van Noppen, 1906.

Blackmun, Ora. *Western North Carolina—Its Mountains and Its People to 1880.* Boone, NC: Appalachian Consortium Press, 1977.

Coates, Albert. *By Her Own Bootstraps: A Saga of Women in North Carolina.* 1975.

Connor, R.D.W. *History of North Carolina. Vol. 1, The Colonial and Revolutionary Period, 1584–1783.* Chicago and New York: The Lewis Publishing Co., 1919.

Federal Writers' Project of the Federal Works Agency Work Projects Administration, The, comp. *North Carolina: The WPA Guide to the Old North State.* Chapel Hill: University of North Carolina Press, 1939.

Hill, Daniel Harvey. *Young People's History of North Carolina.* Raleigh, NC: Alfred Williams & Co., 1916.

Poe, Clarence, and Charles Aycock Poe. *POE-pourri, A North Carolina Cavalcade.* Dallas, TX. Published by Charles Aycock Poe in cooperation with Fine Book Division, Taylor Publishing Co., 1987.

Pope, Larry, ed. *A Pictorial History of Buncombe County.* Asheville, NC: Performance Publications, 1993.

Powell, William S., ed. *Dictionary of North Carolina Biography*, 6 vols. Chapel Hill: University of North Carolina Press, 1994.

Ravi, Jennifer. *Notable North Carolina Women.* Winston-Salem, NC: Bandit Books, 1992.

Ready, Milton. *Asheville, Land of the Sky.* Northridge, CA: Windsor Publications, Inc., 1986.

Rogers, Lou. *Tar Heel Women.* Raleigh, NC: Warren Publishing, 1947.

Sharpe, Bill. *A New Geography of North Carolina.* 4 vols. Raleigh, NC: Sharpe Publishing Company, 1965.

Tessier, Mitzi Schaden. *Asheville, A Pictorical History.* Norfolk, VA: Donning Company, 1982.

Walser, Richard. *Young Readers' Picturebook of Tar Heel Authors.* Raleigh, NC: State Department of Archives and History, 1906.

MARY HOOKS SLOCUMB

Dillard, Richard, "Some North Carolina Heroines of the Revolution," *The North Carolina Booklet*, July 1908.

Flowers, John Baxton III, "Did Polly Slocumb Ride to the Battle of Moore's Creek Bridge?" *Lower Cape Fear Historical Society Bulletin*, February 1976.

Hubbell, S. Michael, "The Mystery of Mary Slocumb," written for the National Park Service, November 27, 1961.

Jaffe, Anthony, "Moore's Creek: A Bridge to the Past," *Wilmington Magazine*, May 1997. (http://wilmmag.wilmington.net/).

Moore, Louis T. *Stories Old and New of the Cape Fear Region.* Wilmington, NC: privately published, 1956.

"Moore's Creek Bridge Historical Site." U.S. Department of the Interior. National Park Service. Washington, D.C.: Government Printing Office, 1983. (http://statelibrary.dcr.state.nc.us/nc/ncsites/moores.htm).

"Polly Slocumb's Own Story of Her Famous Ride," *Fayetteville (NC) Observer*, Special Historical Edition, November, 1939.

"Site for Slocumb Memorial Found," *Goldsboro (NC) News Argus*, May 7, 1970.

Wilson, Ray (descendant of Mary and Ezekiel Slocumb). E-mail correspondence, May 17, 1999.

Wyche, Mary Lewis. *The History of Nursing in North Carolina.* Chapel Hill: University of North Carolina Press, 1938.

BIBLIOGRAPHY

SUSAN TWITTY

"The American Revolution" website, sponsored by Humanities and Social Sciences OnLine (H-Net at Michigan State University), The Omohundro Institute of Early American History and Culture (OIEAHC), National Endowment for the Humanities, PBS Online, and Norwest Corporation. Accessed May 15, 1999. (http://revolution.h-net.msu.edu/).

Beach, Peggy (Cleveland County Public Information Officer). "Battle of Kings Mountain" web page. Accessed May 15, 1999. (http://www.co.cleveland.nc.us/battle_of_kings_mountain.htm).

Carpenter, William Twitty. "Ancestry of William Twitty Carpenter," *The Heritage of Rutherford County, North Carolina, Vol. I.* Winston-Salem, NC: Genealogical Society of Old Tryon County, 1984.

Draper, Lyman C., L.L.D. *King's Mountain and Its Heroes.* Baltimore: Genealogical Publishing Co., Inc., 1983.

Eoz, Zoe. "Tar Heel Tapestries Rewoven," *The Sunday Observer,* May 31, 1925. (North Carolina Collection Clipping File through 1975, UNC Library, Chapel Hill).

Griffin, Clarence W. *History of Old Tryon and Rutherford Counties, North Carolina: 1730–1936.* Asheville, NC: The Miller Printing Company, 1937.

Kings Mountain National Military Park website. Accessed May 1, 1999. (http://www.nps.gov/kimo/).

McCorkle, Lutie Andrews. *Old Time Stories of the Old North State.* Boston: D.C. Heath & Co., 1903.

Middleton, Carol, "The Twitty Family," home page. Accessed February 2, 1999. (http://home.att.net/~c.middleton/TwittylineI.html).

Miller, Susanna. *Will of Susannah Twitty Miller* (originally filed in Book D, Page 37 Wills–Rutherford Co.), copy provided by Michael Feely, descendant.

Our Heritage: A History of Cleveland County. Shelby, NC: The Shelby Daily Star, copyright 1976.

Rutherford County, North Carolina, website, hosted by Internet Blue Ridge. Accessed March 4, 1999.

Simpson, Elizabeth. "The Hero of Graham's Fort." *The State*. September 1, 1972.

ABIGAIL "AUNT ABBY" HOUSE

"Abbie House—An Appreciation," a paper read before the Joseph J. Davis Chapter of the United Daughters of the Confederacy of Louisburg, May 1915 by Elizabeth Person Cooke (North Carolina Collection Clipping File through 1975, UNC Library, Chapel Hill).

Blyth, Ruby Averitt. "Nightingale of Confederacy," *The Raleigh News and Observer*, February 12, 1950.

Clarke, Mary Bayard. "Aunt Abby, The Irrepressible," *The Land We Love*, May–October 1867.

Ellis, Mrs. A.J. "Aunt Abby House Was Mollie Pitcher and Florence Nightingale of the Confederacy," *The Raleigh News and Observer*, April 11, 1926.

Green, A. Wilson (staff historian). "The Battle of Fredericksburg, 1862," Fredericksburg and Spotsylvania National Military Park website. Accessed May 5, 1999. (http://www.nps.gov/frsp/fredhist.htm).

"Marye's Heights," The Civil War Trust website. Copyright 1997. Accessed May 2, 1999. (http:www.civilwar.org/maryes.htm).

Pearce, T.H. "Aunt Abby Finally Got Her Marker," *The State*, May 1974.

———. "Aunt Abby for the Confederacy," *The State*, October 1, 1972.

Whitaker, R.H., "Some Recollections of Aunt Abbey House," *The Raleigh News and Observer*, January 10, 1903.

York, Maury, "Abby House," in *Dictionary of North Carolina Biography*, ed. by William S. Powell. Chapel Hill: University of North Carolina Press, 1994.

HARRIET ANN JACOBS

"Africans in America: America's Journey Through Slavery," The Africans in America website, a production of WGBH Interactive for PBS Online. Copyright 1998, 1999 by WGBH Educational Foundation.

BIBLIOGRAPHY

Davis, James. "Harriet Ann Jacobs," *The Heritage of Blacks in North Carolina*, Vol. I, Charlotte: The North Carolina African-American Heritage Foundation, 1990.

Fleischner, Jennifer. *I Was Born a Slave: The Story of Harriet Jacobs*. Brookfield, CT: The Millbrook Press, 1997.

Jacobs, Harriet. *Incidents in the Life of a Slave Girl: Written by Herself*. Boston: Published for the Author, 1861. Accessed February 21, 1999. (http://www.gc.cc.va.us/~gcadamj/hjhome.htm).

Lyons, Mary E. *Letters from a Slave Girl: The Story of Harriet Jacobs*. New York, NY: Charles Scribner's Sons, 1992.

CORNELIA PHILLIPS SPENCER

"A Sketch of Mrs. Spencer," *Chapel Hill Weekly*, April 25, 1947.

"Bygone Days in Chapel Hill," read before Olla Podrida Club Raleigh by Mrs. George T. Winston, *The Raleigh News and Observer*, April 27, 1902.

Caplan, Gloria. "Mrs. Cornelia P. Spencer Gets Recognition Past Due," *Greensboro Daily News*, May 2, 1948.

"Cornelia Phillips Spencer Named Symbol for Education of Women," *Tar Heel*, March 6, 1932.

Delta Kappa Gamma Society, comp. *Some Pioneer Women Teachers of North Carolina*. North Carolina State Organization, 1955.

"Love and Chapel Hill," *Greensboro Daily News*, January 23, 1962.

Russell, Phillips. *The Woman Who Rang the Bell*. Chapel Hill: University of North Carolina Press, 1949.

"She Was N.C.'s 'Smartest Man'," *Durham Morning Herald*, March 24, 1971.

University of North Carolina at Chapel Hill website. Accessed May 14, 1999. (http://www.unc.edu/).

Wilson, Louis Round. "First Preserver of the University's Environment," *The Chapel Hill Weekly*, February 7, 1971.

———. *Selected Papers of Cornelia Phillips Spencer*. Chapel Hill: The University of North Carolina Press, 1953

Winston, George T., "Recollections of Mrs. Spencer," 1908 (North Carolina Collection Clipping File through 1975, UNC Library, Chapel Hill).

EMELINE JAMISON PIGOTT

Anderson, Lucy London. *North Carolina Women of the Confederacy*. Fayetteville, NC: published by L. L. Anderson (Historian of North Carolina Division), United Daughters of the Confederacy, 1926.

"A History of the 26th North Carolina during the War Between the States," Twenty-Sixth Regiment North Carolina Troops website. Accessed June 1999. (http://63.67.199.67).

Jarrett, Calvin. "The Spy Was A Lady," *Greensboro Daily News*, September 29, 1963. (North Carolina Collection Clipping File through 1975, UNC Library, Chapel Hill).

Jordan, Weymouth T., Jr., comp. *North Carolina Troops, 1861–1865, A Roster*. Vols. 6 and 7-Infantry. Raleigh, NC: State Division of Archives and History, 1979.

Letters to Emeline and Henrietta Pigott, in the Benjamin Royal Papers #2835, Southern Historical Collection, Wilson Library, The University of North Carolina at Chapel Hill.

Manarin, Louis H., comp. *North Carolina Troops, 1861–1865, A Roster*. Vol. 3–Infantry. Raleigh, NC: State Division of Archives and History, 1971.

Rogers, Lou. "Carteret Gave a Heroine," *The Raleigh News and Observer*, November 21, 1948.

Wallace, Mildred. "The Sacrifice or Daring of a Southern Woman During the War Between the States," a paper prepared for the Emeline Pigott chapter of the United Daughters of the Confederacy of Morehead City, in the Benjamin Royal Papers #2835, Southern Historical Collection, Wilson Library, The University of North Carolina at Chapel Hill.

SALLIE SOUTHALL COTTEN

Carraway, Gertrude Sprague. *Carolina Crusaders, History of the North Carolina Federation of Women's Clubs*. New Bern: Owen G. Dunn Company, 1941.

Claggett, Stephen. "North Carolina's First Colonists: 12,000 Years Before Roanoke." Reprinted with permission from *The Li*gature©, NC Division of Archives and History (1986). Revised March 15, 1996. (http://www.arch.dcr.state.nc.us/1stcolo.htm).

Cotten, Bruce. *As We Were, a Personal Sketch of Family Life*. Baltimore: Privately printed for the family only, 1935.

Cotten, Sallie Southall. *History of the North Carolina Federation of Women's Clubs, 1901–1925*. Raleigh: Edwards & Broughton Printing Company, 1925.

———. *The White Doe: The Fate of Virginia Dare*. Philadelphia: Lippincott Co., 1901.

Edwards, Mrs. N. A. (historian), comp. *North Carolina Congress of Parents and Teachers*: History, Vol. I, 1919–1944.

Lawrence, R.C. "A Feminine Hall of Fame," *The State*, November 20, 1943.

"Mother Cotten Taken by Death," *The Raleigh News and Observer*, May 5, 1929.

Stephenson, William. "How Sallie Southall Cotten Brought North Carolina to the Chicago World's Fair of 1893," *The North Carolina Historical Review*, October 1981.

Stephenson, William. *Sallie Southall Cotten: A Woman's Life in North Carolina*. Greenville NC: Pamlico Press, 1987.

DR. ANNIE LOWRIE ALEXANDER

Alexander, John Brevard. *The History of Mecklenburg County from 1740 to 1900*. Charlotte, NC: Observer Printing House, 1902.

Blythe, LeGette. "Old Timers Recall Dr. Annie Alexander," *The Charlotte Observer*, January 21, 1940. (North Carolina Collection Clipping File through 1975, UNC Library, Chapel Hill).

"Dr. Annie Alexander," *The Charlotte Observer*, October 16, 1929. (North Carolina Collection Clipping File through 1975, UNC Library, Chapel Hill).

Dudley, Harold J. "Annie Lowrie Alexander," in *Dictionary of North Carolina Biography*, ed. by William S. Powell. Chapel Hill: University of North Carolina Press, 1994.

Floyd, Barbara (University Archivist, University of Toledo). "From Quackery to Bacteriology: The Emergence of Modern Medicine in 19th Century America." University of Toledo Libraries website. Accessed May 1999. (http://www.cl.utoledo.edu/canaday/quackery/quack-index.html).

"Funeral To Be Held Today for Dr. Alexander," *The Raleigh News and Observer*, October 16, 1929. (North Carolina Collection Clipping File through 1975, UNC Library, Chapel Hill).

"Pay Tribute to Dr. Alexander," *The Charlotte Observer*, October 17, 1929. (North Carolina Collection Clipping File through 1975, UNC Library, Chapel Hill) (ALEXANDER).

Presbyterian Hospital: The Spirit of Caring, 1903–1985. Dallas: Taylor Publishing, 1991.

ADELA F. RUFFIN

Caldwell, Thelma. "YWCA Highlights," from archives of the YWCA, Asheville, NC: 1988.

Cue, Carter (archivist for Winston-Salem State University). Telephone interview, May 28, 1999.

Harrison, Lucy. Transcript of tape recording made October 1993, from archives of the YWCA, Asheville, NC.

Interviews with Helen Bronson, Dolores Carnegie, Lucy Harrison, and Gladys Kennedy, March 1999.

Letter to Bernard Ruffin from Lucy Harrison about Adela Ruffin and the Phyllis Wheatley Branch of the Asheville YWCA. Date unknown.

Minutes of the Board of Directors, YWCA of Asheville, NC. 1920–1946.

Moseley-Edington, Helen. *Angels Unaware: Asheville Women of Color*. Asheville, NC: Home Press, 1996.

"The Municipal Christmas Tree" (photo with cutline), *Asheville Citizen*, December 24, 1925.

BIBLIOGRAPHY

ANNIE WEALTHY HOLLAND

Botsch, Carol Sears. (Faculty Member, History and Political Science), "The Jeanes Supervisors," The University of South Carolina at Aiken website. Accessed May 15, 1999. (http://www.usca.sc.edu/aasc/jeanes.htm).

Newbold, N. C., comp. *Five North Carolina Negro Educators*. Chapel Hill, NC: The University of North Carolina Press, 1939.

"High Tribute to Annie W. Holland," *The Raleigh News and Observer*, January 9, 1934.

Shaber, Sarah R. "Annie Wealthy Holland," in *Dictionary of North Carolina Biography*, ed. by William S. Powell. Chapel Hill: University of North Carolina Press, 1994.

Washington, Booker T. Quoted in "The Hampton Model," Booker T. Washington National Monument Homepage: Accessed May 15, 1999. (http://www.nps.gov/bowa/home.htm).

MARY T. MARTIN SLOOP, M.D.

Alvic, Philis. *The Weaving Room of Crossnore School, Inc.* Avery County Historical Society and Museum: 1998.

"Crossnore School," website, copyright 1997, Crossnore School, Inc., Crossnore, NC (http://www.crossnore.com/).

"Crossnore School Founder Is Named 'Mother of Year,'" *Asheville Citizen*, April 28, 1951.

Fink, Emma Sloop (daughter of Eustace and Mary Sloop). Interview, March 25, 1999.

Kirkland, Winifred. "The Country Gentlewoman," *The Country Gentleman*, March 14, 1925.

Mrs. Mary Martin Sloop Observed Eighty-Second Birthday at Crossnore," *The Gazette*, March 17, 1955.

Sloop, Mary T. Martin, M.D. with Legette Blythe. *Miracle in the Hills*. New York: McGraw-Hill Book Company, Inc., 1953.

Tallent, Jackie (alumnus of Crossnore School). Interview, March 25, 1999.

"Tar Heel Is '51 American Mother," *The Raleigh News and Observer*, May 2, 1951.

Whitt, Anne Hall. *The Suitcases*. Crossnore School Edition. Charlotte: Jostens, 1982.

Yarbrough, Mrs. J.A. "Interesting Carolina People: Dr. Mary Martin Sloop," *The Charlotte Observer*, August 23, 1936.

CHARLOTTE HAWKINS BROWN

"Award Will Go To Dr. Brown," *Greensboro Daily News*, April 10, 1947.

Burns, A.M. III. "Charlotte Hawkins Brown," in *Dictionary of North Carolina Biography*, ed. by William S. Powell. Chapel Hill: University of North Carolina Press, 1994.

"Charlotte Hawkins Brown," Charlotte Hawkins Brown Historical Foundation, Inc., website. Accessed February 21, 1999. (http://www.netpath.net/~chb/).

"Charlotte Hawkins Brown," *Greensboro Daily News*, January 13, 1960.

Daniel, Sadie Iola. "The Early Life of Miss Charlotte Hawkins" and "The Birth and Growth of Palmer Memorial Institute" from *Women Builders*. North Carolina Division of Archives and History: Charlotte Hawkins Brown website. Accessed February 21, 1999. (http://www.ah.dcr.state.nc.us/sections/hs/chb/chb.htm).

"Palmer Founder Succumbs at 77," *Greensboro Daily News*, January 12, 1961.

Saunders, Lucinda Y. "An Idea That Grew from a Shanty into a Million Dollar Project," *Abbott's Monthly*, November 1930.

"The Three Bs of Education: A Holistic Triangle of Ideas," North Carolina Division of Archives and History: Charlotte Hawkins Brown website. Accessed February 21, 1999. (http://www.ah.dcr.state.nc.us/sections/hs/chb/three-bs.htm).

Totton, Ruth (friend of Charlotte Hawkins Brown). Telephone Interview, March 31, 1999.

Wadelington, Charles W. "What One Young African American Woman Could Do: The Story of Dr. Charlotte Hawkins Brown and the Palmer Memorial Institute," *Tar Heel Junior Historian,* Fall 1995. North Carolina Division of Archives and History: Charlotte Hawkins Brown website. Accessed February 21, 1999. (http://www.ah.dcr.state.nc.us/sections/hs/chb/chb.htm).

————. "The Civic Life of Dr. Charlotte Eugenia Hawkins Brown: 1895–1961," North Carolina Division of Archives and History: Charlotte Hawkins Brown website. Accessed February 21, 1999. (http://www.ah.dcr.state.nc.us/sections/hs/chb/chb.htm).

LILLIAN EXUM CLEMENT STAFFORD

Anders, Nancy Lillian Exum Clement Stafford (daughter of Exum Clement). Telephone interviews, January 2 and January 5, 1999.

Announcement of Marriage between Miss L. Exum Clement and Mr. E. E. Stafford, *Asheville Times,* 1921.

Jones, Dr. H. G. "Friends and Attorneys Gave 'Brother Exum' A Chair," *Asheville Times,* May 14, 1980.

"Crowds Pelted Woman Solon," *Asheville Times,* February 15, 1973.

Diary of Lillian Exum Clement Stafford.

Hammerstein, Carol. *Women of the North Carolina General Assembly.* Raleigh: The Foundation for Good Business (issued by Rufus L. Edmisten, Secretary of State), 1995.

"Mrs. Stafford Dies at Home After an Eventful Career," *Asheville Times,* February 22, 1925.

"Our First Woman Legislator" (excerpted from the *Greensboro Daily News,* January 15, 1921). The State, A Weekly Survey of North Carolina, January 27, 1951.

Pope, Larry, ed. *A Pictorial History of Buncombe County.* Asheville, NC: Performance Publications, 1993.

Powell, William S., ed. *Dictionary of North Carolina Biography,* Vol 5. Chapel Hill, NC: University of North Carolina Press, 1994.

Ravi, Jennifer. *Notable North Carolina Women*. Winston-Salem, NC: Bandit Books, 1992.

"Woman Legislator Travels Long Way to Capital," *Asheville Citizen*, May 8, 1960.

MAGGIE AXE WACHACHA

Jackson, Gill. "A Profile Maggie Axe Wachacha," *The Cherokee One Feather*, March 26, 1986.

Journal of Cherokee Studies: Fading Voices, Special Edition. Cherokee, NC: Cherokee Communications, 1991.

"Maggie Wachacha Among Five Who Receive N.C. Distinguished Women Awards," *The Cherokee One Feather*, March 25, 1986.

"Maggie Wachacha, 'Beloved Woman,' dies," *The Cherokee One Feather*, February 10, 1993.

Millsaps, Bill (friend of Maggie Wachacha). E-mail and Interview, March and April, 1999.

Mooney, James. *History, Myths, and Sacred Formulas of the Cherokees* (Originally published in 1891 and 1900 by the Bureau of American Ethnology), Asheville, NC: Historical Images (Bright Mountain Books, Inc.), 1992.

Moore, MariJo. "Remembering Beloved Woman Maggie Wachacha," *Asheville Citizen-Times*, September 6, 1998.

Neely, Sharlotte. *Snowbird Cherokees: People of Persistence*. Athens, GA: The University of Georgia Press, 1991.

Perdue, Theda. *Native Carolinians—The Indians of North Carolina*. Raleigh, NC: Division of Archives and History, North Carolina Department of Cultural Resources, 1985.

Welch, Rick, "Maggie Wachacha Honored at Cherokee-Iroquois Conference," *The Cherokee One Feather*, April 19, 1978.

West, Carolyn (great-granddaughter of Maggie Wachacha). Interview, April 6, 1999.

INDEX

INDEX

INDEX

INDEX

ABOUT THE AUTHOR

Scotti McAuliff Kent grew up in the Midwest, spending the first twenty-six years of her life in Illinois and Minnesota. For the past twenty-three years, she has lived in the mountains of western North Carolina. Although she was not born in "The Old North State," she feels an attachment to her adopted home that family genealogists find easy to explain. It seems she is a descendant of Thomas Talford (sometimes spelled Telford), born in 1740 in Orange County, North Carolina. Another ancestor, Jonas Sparks, resided in Rowan County in the 1760s. Roots of Scotti's family tree also reach deep into the soil of neighboring Tennessee, Virginia, and south Carolina.

Scotti is a freelance writer currently specializing in health care as well as North Carolina history. Her other interests include music, cats, astrology, travel, and writing fiction for middle-grade and young adult readers.

More than Petticoats series

With in-depth and accurate coverage, this series pays tribute to the often unheralded efforts and achievements of the women who settled the West. Each title in the series includes a collection of absorbing biographies and b&w historical photos.

T W O D O T

An Imprint of Falcon Publishing

More than Petticoats:
Remarkable California Women
by Erin H. Turner
$9.95
ISBN 1-56044-859-8

More than Petticoats:
Remarkable Montana Women
by Gayle C. Shirley
$8.95
ISBN 1-56044-363-4

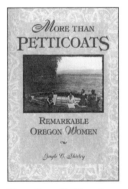

More than Petticoats:
Remarkable Oregon Women
by Gayle C. Shirley
$9.95
ISBN 1-56044-668-4

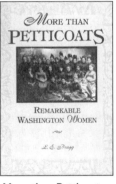

More than Petticoats:
Remarkable Washington Women
by L.E. Bragg
$9.95
ISBN 1-56044-667-6

TwoDot features books that celebrate and interpret the rich culture and history of regional America.

To order check with your local bookseller or call Falcon at **1-800-582-2665**. *Ask for a FREE catalog featuring a complete list of titles on nature, outdoor recreation, travel and the West.*

www.falconbooks.com

FALCON®

It Happened in *Series from TwoDot Books*

An imprint of Falcon Publishing

TWODOT

Featured in this series are fascinating stories about events that helped shape each state's history. Written in a lively, easy-to-read style, each book features about 30 stories for history buffs of all ages. Entertaining and informative, each book is 6x9", features b&w illustrations, and is only **$9.95.**

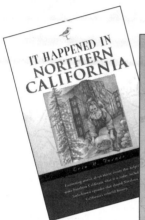
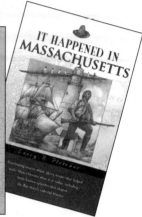

It Happened in Northern California
by Erin H. Turner
$8.95
ISBN 1-56044-844-X

It Happened in Arizona
by James A. Crutchfield
$8.95
ISBN 1-56044-264-6

It Happened in Massachusetts
by Larry B. Pletcher
$9.95
ISBN 1-56044-846-6

Also Available:

It Happened in Colorado
It Happened in Georgia
It Happened in Montana
It Happened in New Mexico
It Happened in Oregon
It Happened in Southern California
It Happened in Texas
It Happened in Utah
It Happened in Washington

TwoDot features books that celebrate and interpret the rich culture and history of regional America.

To order check with your local bookseller or call Falcon at **1-800-582-2665.**
Ask for a FREE catalog featuring a complete list of titles on nature, outdoor recreation, travel and the West.

www.falconbooks.com

FALCON®